Parenting a College Student

Copyright © 2023 by F. J. Talley

All rights reserved. No part of this book may be reproduced or used in any manner without written permission of the copyright owner except for the use of quotations in a book review. For more information, address: fjtalleyauthor@gmail.com.

First paperback edition June 2023

Cover design by GetCovers

Edited by Natalie Silver

Formatting by James Brewster

ISBN 978-0-9996012-5-9 (paperback)

www.collegeandparents.com

Parenting a College Student

F. J. Talley

Contents

Introduction 1

Chapter 1 - Background 9

Chapter 2 - How Colleges Work 21

Chapter 3 - Majors and Minors 29

Chapter 4 - Choosing a College 35

Chapter 5 - Paying for College 51

Chapter 6 - The Decision 59

Chapter 7 - Transitioning to College 67

Chapter 8 - Living Away from Home 77

Chapter 9 - Life in a Diverse Community 83

Chapter 10 - Safety and Other Things You Worry About 93

Chapter 11 - Academic Success in College 101

Chapter 12 - Taking Notes in College 111

Chapter 13 - A Typical Day 121

Chapter 14 - Beyond the Classroom 127

Chapter 15 - Intercollegiate Athletics 131

Chapter 16 - Helping Them Adult on Campus 137

Chapter 17 - Finding Help in College 145

Chapter 18 - Experiential Learning 153

Chapter 19 - Study Abroad 157

Chapter 20 - Alternate Paths 161

Chapter 21 - After College 167

Appendix 173

Meet the Author 174

Introduction

Why this book? The answer is simple. Every one of us who has a son or daughter (or other family member) in college wants that person to succeed. Yet the way we help them succeed is different in college from the way it was in high school. Parents often bristle when college administrators and faculty say, "We can't talk to you since your student is now an adult." Oh, *really?* That may not be the way *you* see them.

Well, the colleges are right, and yet they're wrong, too. Your son will always be your son, your daughter will always be your daughter, and you want nothing for them but happiness and success.

There are countless websites and books to help college students succeed: I've read many of them myself while working in higher education. But few focus on the experiences and concerns of parents and family members. That's why I started collegeandparents.com.

Before we get into the book itself, it might be helpful to address the elephant in the room, which is *why go to college at all?* People in a variety of fields have succeeded without college degrees, such as industry giants Bill Gates or Steve Jobs who dropped out of college.[1] There are also other entrepreneurs who have made a significant impact and earned financial wealth without attending or completing college.

Many of you reading this book may not have college degrees either and are happy with your lives as they are. I should clarify here that when I refer to going to college, it's to pursue an associate's, bachelor's, or other advanced degree. I'm not referring to the career programs offered by community colleges or trade schools, in fields such as auto mechanics, cosmetology, or culinary arts. This book addresses those fields only in passing as they are often part of a community college's wide offerings, but there are several reasons why students should consider attending two- and four-year colleges.

My father—who was a very intelligent man—was born in 1925 and dropped out of high school sometime in his sophomore or junior year. After five years in the army during World War II, he became a butcher and then began working as a meat inspector with the United States Department of Agriculture. He went on to supervise other inspectors and then finished his career as the assistant officer in charge for the northeast region (twelve states plus DC) for meat law investigation. That was a pretty big job, and he was a GS-12 when he retired in 1980. But that meat inspector job that he secured with less than a high school education? That now requires a master's degree just to *start*. So, one reason for pursuing a college education is the fact that many fields—even those that didn't need them before—now require a college degree to enter. When I completed high school, people could enter the police academy and then get hired as officers after completion, with no college background. That's far less common today, even for very small or rural communities. The same applies to nurses, who fifty years ago might graduate from a one-year hospital program and be set for life. Now, community colleges offer associate degree registered nurse programs, but with the nationwide push for the Bachelor of Science in Nursing, aspiring nurses will have to earn a bachelor's degree for the employment options they want. In short, your student will have many more options by earning a college degree than they will have without them.

Another important reason is earning potential. According to the Association of Public and Land-Grant Universities, over a lifetime, the average high school graduate will earn $1,304,000 dollars. This is from a study conducted in 2013 by the Georgetown University Center on Education and the Workforce, but the results parallel those from previous studies of this type. For high school dropouts, that number is decidedly less, but for students with a bachelor's degree, that lifetime earnings figure jumps to $2,268,000 and rises to $2,671,000 for those with a master's degree.[2]

Another factor that points to the value of a college degree is the increasing mobility of people, at least within the United States. It's far less common today for people to work at the same company for their entire careers. Students who have the credentials--often a bachelor's degree--are better prepared to move their work to other cities or states or to pursue their career online or remotely.

In short, your student will have more options and be better able to thrive in the work world of tomorrow with credentials past high school.

And make no mistake: those students who choose to enlist in the military first *are* getting advanced training. Soldiers, sailors, and marines often complete their degrees while enlisted so their options after their enlistment or retirement are broader than they would be otherwise.

Another significant benefit to earning a college degree, particularly at the bachelor's level, is to insulate people from economic hardship, with those holding a bachelor's degree or higher having the lowest levels of unemployment.[3]

Earnings and unemployment rates by educational attainment, 2021

Educational attainment	Median usual weekly earnings	Unemployment rate
Doctoral degree	$1,909	1.5%
Professional degree	1,924	1.8
Master's degree	1,574	2.6
Bachelor's degree	1,334	3.5
Associate's degree	963	4.6
Some college, no degree	899	5.5
High school diploma	809	6.2
Less than a high school diploma	626	8.3

Note: Data are for persons age 25 and over. Earnings are for full-time wage and salary workers.
Source: U.S. Bureau of Labor Statistics, Current Population Survey.

Figure 1. Jobless Rates by Education Level in the Twenty-First Century

Those who advocate attending college often cite increased career opportunities, higher lifetime job earnings, and a greater likelihood to have positions with benefits, such as sick leave, health insurance, life insurance, and so forth.[4] Education leads to lower unemployment, increased job security, and personal satisfaction, which are positive reasons to attend and graduate from college. Proponents of a traditional college education also point to the networking opportunities during and right after college that lead to greater mobility and the ability to weather short-term economic downturns.

Despite all this evidence, more and more people today question the value of a higher education, citing statistics on the high amount of debt students carry. As noted on the US News and World Report website, the average student loan debt for college students graduating in 2020 was $29,900.[5] Further, some cite the National Center for Education Statistics, which found "that only 62% of college students finish their degree within six years," missing the benefits of college altogether.[6,7] These concerns are worth considering. Student loan debt continues to rise, and college graduates pay off those debts well into their professional career. And if you Google "Is college worth it?," half of the responses you see focus on student loan debt.

Colleges and universities are attempting to respond to the high costs of tuition and rising student debt. However, only those who graduate from college reap these benefits: without a degree, there is little long-term benefit.[7] Further, while college graduates often out earn those with only high school diplomas, the difference depends on the field the student enters. For example, for graduates in science, technology, engineering, and mathematics, the difference is significant over their peers who didn't attend college. For students pursuing majors such as English and the arts, the difference is far less. On top of this is the increasing expectation that college will prepare graduates for specific careers, putting more pressure on career centers to transform what they do and how they do it. Colleges have been responding to this. Whether it's the "Careers in" series at the University of Chicago or required career sections of freshman experience courses around the country, many colleges are increasing career-related activities for their students to help them make the transition from college to the world of work.[8]

Yet some point out that colleges shouldn't prepare graduates for specific careers for several good reasons. First, the career they may end up in *may not exist yet*. Second, it's likely that graduates will enter an economy where they won't remain in the same job or career for their entire working lives.[9] Colleges might say that giving students skills they can apply to a variety of jobs and resources to shift and retool themselves is far more important than single-path career preparation.

Where does this leave you as the parent or family member of a college student? If you're like many of us, you're anxious and unsure. That's not a bad thing: being a little unsure means you're open to learning how to help your student make the best possible choice for college and help them succeed and thrive. That's why I wrote this book.

The chapters in this book cover helping your student prepare for college, searching and finding the right college, and figuring out how to finance a college education. There are also chapters on how colleges operate, the changes students go through while in college, and the challenges they face. I will also focus on tips and tricks you can use with your student so they get the help they need when they're struggling and how they can benefit the most from what their college offers. In every section, you'll see references to reputable documents and websites I've found that back up what I'm saying.

I'll also provide you with my perspective and reflections that may lower your anxiety as you sit on the sidelines hoping your student makes the right decisions, all the while knowing you can't make those decisions for them. It's like watching your daughter on the soccer field when she was nine and hoping she wouldn't move the wrong way and let the ball into her goal. We sit on the sidelines as parents and family members supporting our athletes with butterflies in our stomachs until the game is over. When your student goes to college, the butterflies come back, and those butterflies may resurface with every tearful phone call we receive from our struggling college student. The fact is most students can and will navigate these challenges. As hard as they may seem when they're happening, as parents or family members, you'll be navigating these challenges, too.

And when you look back four years later, you will finally appreciate the beauty of butterflies again.

References

1. Knerl, L. (2018). *Can You Succeed without College? Yes, but It's Complicated.* Bachelor's Degree Completion. https://www.northeastern.edu/bachelors-completion/news/succeeding-without-college/

2. Carnevale, A., Rose, S., & Cheah, B. (2013). Review of *The College Payoff: Education, Occupations, Lifetime Earnings.* The Georgetown University Center on Education and the Workforce.

3. U.S. Bureau of Labor Statistics. (2022, May). *Education pays, 2021 : Career Outlook: U.S. Bureau of Labor Statistics.* Www.bls.gov. https://www.bls.gov/careeroutlook/2022/data-on-display/education-pays.htm

4. Loveless, B. (2018). *Benefits of Earning a College Degree.* Educationcorner.com. https://www.educationcorner.com/benefit-of-earning-a-college-degree.html

5. Kerr, E. (2020, September 15). *See 10 Years of Average Total Student Loan Debt.* US News & World Report. https://www.usnews.com/education/best-colleges/paying-for-college/articles/see-how-student-loan-borrowing-has-risen-in-10-years

6. Oneal, A. (2018). *Is College Worth It?* Ramsey. https://www.daveramsey.com/blog/is-college-worth-it.

7. *Is College Worth It? Going Beyond Averages.* (2012). Third Way. https://www.thirdway.org/report/is-college-worth-it-going-beyond-averages

8. Greeley, M. (2014). *How Colleges Help Students Gear Up for Jobs.* US News & World Report. https://www.usnews.com/education/best-

colleges/articles/2019-09-09/how-colleges-help-students-gear-up-for-jobs

9. PBS NewsHour. (2018, December 6). *How Colleges Are Preparing Students for Jobs That Don't Exist Yet*. PBS NewsHour. https://www.pbs.org/newshour/economy/making-sense/how-colleges-are-preparing-students-for-jobs-that-dont-exist-yet

Chapter 1 - Background

The move from being the parent of a high school student to the parent of a college student is a much bigger step than most people realize. When your student was enrolled in high school, you served as their primary advocate and gatekeeper. When anything went wrong in school, such as a bad grade, poor attendance, or missing or late homework, you heard about it. Many school systems across the country have online systems where parents can check on their student's academic progress, assignment by assignment. These tools can keep parents informed on their student's progress during the academic year. It can also alert parents when a teacher isn't submitting grades in a timely fashion.

This system is in place because while your student is in high school, you are ultimately responsible for them since they're minors. Certainly, their grades are their responsibility, but some states or cities penalize parents if students act out in school or skip school repeatedly.[1] This social contract runs from kindergarten through high school. It's familiar and what we expect from education for our children.

Many parents don't realize that when students go to college, the relationships change between the student, the college, and them. In 1961, Eric Berne wrote a book about transactional analysis, or TA. Berne explained how when we communicate, we are doing so as either a parent, a child, or an adult, and the person we're speaking with responds as either a parent, a child, or an adult.[2] Think about that. When we tell our child to put on a sweater before going outside, we're acting as a parent speaking with a child. For a five-year-old that's fine. But imagine that same conversation with a sixteen-year-old. Telling a teenager anything is a chore, but telling them how to dress? Good luck. You're unlikely to hear a "Yes, Mom." You'll probably see their eyes roll instead. You want them to put on a sweater because it's cold outside, but a sixteen-year-old *knows* it's cold outside and, further, knows how cold it has to be for them to put on a sweater or jacket on their own. Were you to insist they wear a sweater or jacket, that might cause a child-like response, where the teenager shrugs, takes the sweater, and, once they're out of your sight, rolls it up and places it in their backpack—even if it's freezing outside—just to show you they won't do what you tell them to do just because you tell them to do it.

Instead of telling a teenager to put on a sweater, we're likely to get a better response by saying, "It's about forty degrees outside and it feels colder than it looks." A teenager would hear that, ponder if forty degrees is cold enough for a sweater or jacket, and answer with something like, "It'll be all right, especially once it warms up." That's a fine adult response: they considered what you said, evaluated it on their own terms, then gave a considered answer.

The challenge when our children head to college is to move toward more adult/adult conversations and interactions. That's even harder since many of the tools we had in K-12 education—such as those grade-tracking programs—dry up the minute they start college. So, how can you still be an engaged parent when you're stripped of your familiar toolkit?

A New Role for Parents

Jim Burns addresses this in his article "The Changing Role for Parents of College Students." He refers to the new role for parents as that of an advisor, rather than of the conductor or director. As Burns explains it:

How this change to an advisor role works out in real life depends largely upon the groundwork you're laid up until now. Parents who have maintained a high degree of control over their teenager during the high school years will have a different experience than the parents who have slowly but steadily allowed their child to become more independent. The point for parents to focus on, regardless of previous parenting styles, is to help your son or daughter make a successful transition to the more independent lifestyle students experience on college campuses.³

I call this becoming a consultant to your student and discuss that on my website, collegeandparents.com.⁴

Burns further says—and I agree—that even with this change in role, we are parents in perpetuity, but the parenting role evolves and grows just as our children grow throughout their lifetimes. We wouldn't dream of telling our thirty-year-old son to put on a sweater because it's cold outside, would we? If not, when did we decide that was his decision to make, rather than ours? A convenient time for that transition is when our students go to college, the first time when they are expected to make adult decisions consistently.

Some parents lament this on several levels. First, they worry that their student—who hasn't made his bed well in eighteen years—isn't ready to make adult decisions. Perhaps they're right, and no college or university expects that eighteen-to-twenty-two-year-old college students will make the same mature decisions their parents do. That's why so many staff members at colleges focus on helping students through that mature decision-making process as young adults, not as older kids. The student who hasn't made his bed may need more shepherding toward adulthood than others, however.⁵

Another point parents raise is that they are the primary people paying for their student's education. Fair enough. But the college doesn't care who pays the bill, they care only that the bill gets paid. Further, they have to treat every student the same, whether their parents are footing the bill or not.

This doesn't mean you have no legitimate role as the parents of a college student. Your student will call and consult with you throughout college, but their interactions with you will be different. They'll call you because they'll feel they're being treated poorly by a faculty member in their psychology class, they're stressing out about an upcoming exam in math, they feel betrayed by a new friend, or they didn't get into their fraternity or sorority of choice. And they seldom bother to update you when those situations are resolved.

Knowing how to respond to these concerns is one of the aims of this book.

Make no mistake: parenting a college student isn't any easier than parenting a five-year-old, but the stakes are bigger and much more expensive. This book will teach you how to approach this new role.

Ready or Not

The first step in helping your student succeed in college is knowing if they're ready in the first place.[6] Readiness is important for many things in life: figuring out if they're ready for a two-wheeled bike or their driver's license are two situations that come to mind. The same goes for college. How can you be sure your student is ready for college, given that their grades and standardized test scores are only part of this equation? Let's assume your student is reasonably intelligent: they can read, know the basics of studying, and can string words together into a decent essay. They may also enjoy learning and the opportunity to debate and discuss important topics in a course or with friends. If your student has these qualities, they're in good shape. But beyond this baseline, I believe there are several factors to determine if your student is ready for college. The first is the drive to succeed, and the second is the willingness to ask for and receive help along the way.

The drive to succeed is tough to measure, since every student will tell you they want to succeed. Who wouldn't say that if asked? I define it as a desire to succeed combined with a good work ethic. This means they now have to work hard and sometimes skip doing the things they want to do such as spending time with friends to read a difficult section of a college textbook. Most students will say they have a good work ethic, yet you'd be surprised by the number of students who say they have drive but do little to make success happen. A student who starts the semester by skipping classes, for example, isn't showing a drive to succeed.

I've noticed that with some of my students. For example, many professors tell students in their course syllabus that they can miss up to four classes during the semester until those absences impact their grade. I've had students skip one class a week for four weeks early in the semester because "it doesn't count until the fifth absence, anyway." This student is not ready for college, because instead of seeing the absences as available for unavoidable things such as illness or to let them prepare for a tough exam in another course, they instead see it as a "get out of jail free card." That's not adult-level thinking, and that student is not showing a drive to succeed. When I've spoken to these students, I ask, "If you've used up your four absences, what happens if you get sick later in the semester and can't go to class?" Their pleas of "well, the professor will cut me a break" will fall on deaf ears. The professor told them how they're giving them a break by not counting their first four absences against them. The professor is under no obligation to cut them any more breaks. The student usually gives me a blank look after I tell them that.

The willingness to ask for and receive help is incredibly important, too, and a tougher one to teach students. We push our students to work hard while they're in high school, though many of them find high school quite easy. We show them the value of working hard and not giving up, and they take these lessons to heart. That's good, since working hard is a part of adult life. However, it can be hard for a young adult to know when taking a step back—either by asking for help or choosing to drop a course—is the smart thing to do, because we've programmed them into believing that giving up or retreating is a sign of failure. Most of us accept help or instruction along the way to improve, and we think nothing of offering help to others. But our students aren't mature enough to understand that, and they don't want to disappoint their parents by dropping a course or calling for help. They see accepting help as a sign of weakness. Instead, it is a sign of strength, and an important factor in ongoing college success.

I worked with a student years ago who I'll call Sam. Sam was on academic probation because of poor first semester grades. He was a pleasant young man with a strong work ethic, who had one particular academic challenge: he could read well, but he was slower than most. On one of his assignments, he couldn't read all the materials in time to write a good essay, so he turned in just an outline and a few paragraphs, far less than what was required. When I asked Sam if he had spoken with his professor about his reading challenge or the assignment, he said he hadn't because "then she'll think I'm stupid." I responded with "well, now she thinks you don't care about her class: is that what you want?" Sam said he didn't and agreed to go with me to visit the professor's office to speak with her. Halfway there, he stopped and gave me an angry look: he did *not* want to go. At the time, I was a vice president and dean of students at the college, so he had little choice. He sighed and continued walking. When we arrived, I gave the instructor a brief introduction, and then Sam told her about his reading challenge and why his essay was so poor. The professor was a champ: she asked him to sit so they could discuss how she could help him and began mapping out how they could work together for the rest of the semester. Sam was floored. He never thought she'd be so nice to him. That's the first time Sam realized that asking for help coupled with his work ethic would help him succeed in college. And whenever students in that class said they were struggling, he was the first to suggest that they speak with the professor.

I saw the same willingness with one of my students years later. This student had the same "I want to do this on my own" attitude. The difference with her was when someone suggested she try something new, such as applying for a position as a resident assistant or another campus leadership position, she'd often say, "I don't know if I can do that." Then she would look at me and ask: "Would you help me?" My answer was always yes, and this student succeeded because she knew getting help along the way would support her success. She graduated in four years and, while she was the middle of three siblings, she was the first to earn a bachelor's degree.

How Do You and They Define Success?

One area of conflict between parents and students is with how each defines success. For example, is earning a C in a challenging course good enough? Some parents say yes and others no. And it's interesting to see that sometimes, the opposite is the case. The C in a challenging course may be good enough for the parent who knows how hard their student had to work to earn that grade, but the student feels like a failure for not earning a B. The takeaway? Discuss with your student what success in college means long before they walk onto campus.

Another measure of success is to graduate—that's it, just graduate. Fewer than half of the people who start college in a given year graduate in four years, and that number doesn't increase much after six years. A student may learn a great deal in six years at school without earning a degree and have a straight-B average. However, they can never say they graduated from University X on their resume. Further, if they need a bachelor's degree to qualify for a job, they'll never have it, no matter their grade point average.

On the other hand, the student who barely scraped by with a straight C average from University X earned that credential and it can never be taken away. Not that students shouldn't work hard to earn high grades; it's keeping in perspective that five years after graduation, their grade point average will matter far less than the fact that they earned the degree. The phrase students often use is "C's get degrees." I don't like the phrase much, but it's accurate. I repeat the phrase to students who are struggling in a course and know they'll only earn a C in it. My reminder? They passed the course: move on to the next one.

An additional measure of success is how much the student grows while in college. Expect that when your student comes home for Thanksgiving, you'll see someone who looks different: taller, older, and more in command of themselves. They may also come home looking quite different: different hair color, different hair style, piercings, tattoos, and so forth. This may be a shock, but that's what is *supposed* to happen. We often talk about student growth along several dimensions using the SPICES acronym. They will grow socially, physically, intellectually, culturally, emotionally, and spiritually. For family members whose student attends a residential college, many of the activities your student will attend in their residence hall will be planned with this SPICES acronym in mind. These aren't just social activities: they also challenge students to grow in terms of their cultural understanding, become more accomplished physically, and help them become successful in the classroom. We'll expand more on this in a later chapter.

I recall an interesting phone call from my daughter that illustrated her emotional growth. She called me one evening because she and some of her friends were concerned about another friend who they believed was in an abusive relationship. They thought the friend's boyfriend was too controlling. Some of the concerns my daughter and her friends mentioned included the boyfriend looking at who his girlfriend texted, demanding that she tell him where she was going, who she was spending time with, and so forth. This caused the girlfriend a high level of stress, resulting in fits of crying and her being unable to attend class because of her depression. My daughter called me and placed the phone on speaker. Then, she and two of her friends and I chatted about the ways they could approach their friend to get her out of the abusive relationship and what help they might ask for from campus authorities. What they were struggling with emotionally was trying to be supportive of their friend while helping her stay in control of her life. That may seem like a small distinction, but people in abusive relationships don't need someone else taking control from them: they need to find the support to make and carry out decisions on their own, and that's what my daughter and her friends needed to learn. My conversation that evening was a perfect example of adult-adult interactions among the four of us and a great illustration of the emotional growth that college students should engage in.

Of course, their university has people on staff who could have helped them answer and probe their concerns as well I could. My daughter trusted me, however, and knew that I had expertise in these issues because of my background: she just used the closest resource she had. She's since had similar conversations with college staff once she got to know them. And it's a measure of success that my daughter grew along all of the SPICES dimensions. Your student can as well.

What Makes Student Success Happen?

Student learning—which leads to student success—happens in many ways, some planned and some spontaneous. Many well-known scholars such as Vincent Tinto, Ernest Pascarella, and Patrick Terenzini have suggested that the two most important factors are academic integration and social integration. Let me break that down for you. Academic integration is how well a student's academic behaviors match what the college expects of them. Colleges expect students to attend class, complete their assignments on time, engage in class discussions, and not cheat, for example. Some schools also require undergraduates to complete a thesis or some sort of senior capstone experience in order to graduate. So, students who don't attend class regularly, cheat, or do sloppy and unscholarly research would not be well integrated academically.[7,8]

Social integration is trickier: it's how well a student's social behaviors match what the college expects of them. Common social expectations include interacting in positive ways with other students, engaging with people from a variety of backgrounds, going to social activities put on by the college, and joining and taking part in clubs. But it goes beyond that since these social expectations are often specific to institutional types or individual schools. For example, a medium-size state institution may have no expectation that students attend chapel, but a religious private institution may require daily chapel attendance. Some schools require men to wear collared shirts to class and for women to wear dresses or skirts unless they're in their residence hall. Men who object to these rules and push the limits by wearing T-shirts to class or women who wear slacks in the dining hall wouldn't be well integrated into a school with a strict dress code. But those same students might fit in beautifully at another college or university. They would be poorly socially integrated with the first institution but do well with the second. Social integration doesn't hold one type of institution as good or bad: the point is how well the student fits socially within the institution.

It's often a measure of social integration that determines the "fit" students have with a particular school, which I'll discuss in a later chapter.

Another factor that leads to student success is high expectations of students—by themselves and others—tempered with reality. Here's what I mean. Research has shown that when we present students with high expectations, and support them in meeting those expectations, they often rise to the challenge.[9] Yet we should recognize that when the academic goals students have don't fit their skills or performance, no amount of high expectations and support—

in the short term—will help them succeed. That's when they need a reality check.

One of my past students had completed four years of college but was still at least a year and a half away from completing her bachelor's in biochemistry. She retook several courses two or three times, which for most of us would tell us we're in the wrong major. The student, her advisor, and I discussed this on two occasions, and we encouraged the student to focus more on finishing a degree, rather than one specifically in biochemistry. The catch was that she had always wanted to be a pharmacist, and that's what her parents sent her to college to do. The student also recognized that given her grade point average and repeating essential science courses two or three times, she would never be admitted to pharmacy school. We gave her the dose of reality she needed to consider a different major. That was a painful but necessary discussion for her. I had a similar discussion with another student at the end of her sophomore year. When she changed her major, it was like the lights came on. She graduated on time, and for her senior year, she hit the dean's list twice—her only times on the dean's list—and earned all A's for her final semester. With her bachelor's degree, she's now ready to launch. Your student can, too.

In Brief

Look to build more adult/adult interactions with your student.

Embrace becoming your student's primary life consultant.

Remember that you still have a role with your student—but that it will be different.

Help your student assess how ready they are for college, and why they're going.

Talk with your student about what success in college looks like and strive to create a common understanding of it.

Remember that success in college isn't just in the classroom.

References

1. *Inexcusable Absences*. (2015, March 6). The New Republic. https://newrepublic.com/article/121186/truancy-laws-unfairly-attack-poor-children-and-parents

2. Berne, E. (1961). Review of *Transactional Analysis in Psychotherapy*. Castle Books.

3. Burns, J. (2012, April 16). Review of *The Changing Role for Parents of College Students*. HomeWord.com.

4. Talley, F. J. (2018, July 8). *Becoming a Consultant to your Student*. Helping Your College Student Succeed. http://www.collegeandparents.com/2018/07/08/becoming-a-consultant-to-your-student/

5. *Are Today's Students Really Ready for College, Work and Life?* (2017, March 15). Getting Smart. https://www.gettingsmart.com/2017/03/students-really-ready-college-work-life/

6. *Telltale Signs of College Readiness and How to Instill It When Lacking*. (n.d.). Verywell Family. https://www.verywellfamily.com/signs-your-high-school-senior-is-ready-for-college-4171729

7. Tinto, V. (2012). *Leaving College: Rethinking the Causes and Cures of Student Attrition*. University of Chicago Press; .

8. Pascarella, E. T., & Terenzini, P. T. (2005). *How College Affects Students. Volume 2: A Third Decade of Research*. Jossey-Bass.

9. Community College Survey of Student Engagement (CCSSE). (2008). *High Expectations and High Support*. The University of Texas at Austin, Community College Leadership Program.

Chapter 2 - How Colleges Work

Colleges are complex organizations that can be hard to understand. Here are some insights into the place your student will be spending a great deal of time at in the next few years.

There are more than 4,200 colleges and universities in the United States alone. Of these, 1,626 are public—supported in part by the government—and 1,687 are independent nonprofit (we often refer to them as "private"), meaning they operate separately from direct government aid, with the remainder being for-profit colleges.[1] Many private colleges and universities receive money from the government, but these are in the form of grants for specific purposes, rather than a regular allocation. And many public colleges receive far less funding than you'd think. For example, Temple University in Philadelphia receives only 10 percent of its funding from the Commonwealth of Pennsylvania.[2] The same can be said of the state's flagship public university, Penn State. Many of these schools are referred to as "state related" these days because of how little financial support they receive from public sources.[3]

The first thing you and your student may see is that independent colleges cost more. Independent college tuition (not including room and board) may be well over $30,000 per year, compared to an average of $9,970 for public colleges, though public college tuition varies from state to state and school to school.[4]

Different Options for Undergraduate Education

Schools that offer only associate's degrees, certificates, and career training are known as community colleges, and in 2020, almost half of all students enrolled in American higher education attended community colleges. That percentage has remained steady for about twenty years. So, if your student chooses a community college, they're in good company. Some reasons for attending a community college are purely financial: they usually cost much less than a comparable public four-year college. And since very few of them have residence halls, your student would normally commute from home, saving room and board costs.

A nonfinancial reason to attend a community college, however, is that the courses in community colleges fulfill the same basic learning goals as in four-year schools, and, beyond that, many have class sizes that are smaller than those of four-year schools. Also, community college faculty are particularly focused on teaching, rather than on research. There's nothing wrong with research, which is doing more work to advance knowledge in a variety of fields. That's what faculty members at four-year colleges and larger universities do as a significant part of their job. But in the case of community colleges, faculty are focused primarily on teaching, which means they get even more practice teaching to a wide variety of learning styles and experiences. Choosing a community college is not settling for an inferior education.[5,6]

Then there are four-year colleges and universities. When we think about our students "going to college," we tend to think about them going away to a place with ivy-covered walls in a college town. That's what we see on TV and in the movies. Some colleges have fewer than five thousand students, and even if they say they're "universities," they may still have the smaller classes we associate with colleges. These smaller colleges can be public or independent. Universities are generally much larger, with groups of majors organized into schools or colleges. The University of Maryland, for example, has the School of Engineering, the College of Arts and Humanities, and many others. These schools and colleges act like small colleges in themselves, with their own faculty and buildings. Students in larger universities often have larger class sizes than at small colleges, but they have the advantage of a richer campus life offering students more options.

Administrative Areas

Within colleges and universities are other departments separate from learning. For example, there are whole divisions focused solely on getting your student to enroll and begin with the proper amount of financial aid. These are referred to as enrollment management units. Another unit is student affairs, which includes most out-of-classroom activities. These encompass residence halls, student activities, student government, clubs and organizations, wellness, and, sometimes, athletics. These departments are designed to help your student learn outside the classroom to support their overall growth. Another college division is for business, including where you pay tuition. This division may also include the bookstore and food services, which are important supports to the well-being of your student, both academically and physically.[7,8]

The College Classroom

College classrooms feel quite different from high school classrooms. Many will be laid out in a circle rather than in rows, but that doesn't matter. There are three primary teaching formats for college courses.

The first is lecture, where a professor is often speaking and teaching class material. This is more teacher focused.

The second format is a discussion classroom, which is more student or learner focused. In this format, much of the class consists of the instructor asking questions that spark discussion and back-and-forth dialogue among the students.

A third common format for college classes is the laboratory classroom, where students are working on projects and assignments in a controlled lab environment. Not surprisingly, laboratory classes are often in the sciences.[9,10]

Many college courses use a combination of these techniques, especially the first two. That's the case for my classes. And when I teach Social Psychology, I use all three techniques. I know few faculty members who teach using lecture alone these days.

Another difference between high school and college classes is that college students seldom use worksheets during class. Rather, the faculty member asks students questions that help clarify the most important points in the reading the students just completed. For example, I might assign a chapter or two, or maybe two separate readings between classes. I expect that all of the students have completed the reading *before* the next class. When I ask what questions the students have based on the reading, I expect—sometimes without success—that *someone* will raise a question or comment. And once I ask if they have questions, I'll likely wait much longer for students to answer than I might in a high school classroom.

Here's another important difference between high school and college: in college, students often aren't required to attend all of their classes. This means the responsibility for learning and performing rests primarily on the student. And if they don't engage with the material by asking questions, doing the reading, and participating in class discussions, that's on them.

This is one of the toughest things for first-year students to grasp. Since college classes don't offer many chances for evaluation, such as tests and papers, students can find themselves "behind" pretty quickly. They are behind by not keeping up with the reading and making sure they understand it or because they don't receive daily feedback from their professors and *they may learn that too late*. This is why focusing on their academics as soon as they arrive is so important in college. Students won't have five or six exams to figure out what the professor wants: they should try to hit it out of the park every time. And if they don't, they should follow up with the professor immediately. They also shouldn't count on having their lowest exam score dropped to save their grade. What if they don't do well on more than one? Encourage your student to start off strong in every single class.

The Syllabus

The syllabus is the contract between the student and the faculty member, which outlines the readings, assignments, expectations, and grading practices for the course. A good syllabus tells students what's expected for their success in the course and lays out a schedule of readings and evaluations so students can prepare for them. Everything should be in there. I reorganized my syllabus in 2021 into a Google site so students can access it more easily, and in a more student-friendly manner. But don't look for the traditional syllabus—be it passed out in class or sent as a Word document through email—to go away soon.[11]

Active Learning

I've alluded to this before: college students must be actively engaged and direct their own learning. They should be clear about what they want to learn and prod their professors to help them learn it. College faculty won't ram information down their throats against their will. Instead, faculty ask questions to help students make connections in their minds and to learn at a deeper level.[12,13]

A good example of this is my recent course, Strategic Nonviolence and Civil Disobedience, which I adapted almost wholesale from a colleague in Pennsylvania. During our final two class days, I asked the students—after some readings and viewing selected videos—to tell me why the mass movements for greater liberty in two countries, Myanmar/Burma in 1989 and China in 1989, didn't succeed. I was thrilled that every student identified the answers based on the course material and discussions almost immediately. These were the best days of the course: my students *got* it.

Another feature that confuses parents is the fact that students take many courses that aren't in their major field of study. These courses may be in the humanities, social sciences, natural sciences, or mathematics. Collectively, these courses are often known as general education. They represent the knowledge that colleges and universities say students should have as educated people. You'll find many variations in general education requirements around the country, and your student's college will have its own. So long as your student listens to their advisor, but also examines and studies the college catalog, they should be fine with the courses they choose, be they in general education or in their major or minor fields of study.[14,15]

Working with Faculty

A final point about faculty: as different as they may be from high school faculty, they want your student to succeed, though your student may not see it that way. Encourage your student to connect with each of their professors. They should know their faculty members' office location and go there to clarify information and ask questions on a regular basis. Your student should be someone who faculty members know for the right reasons.

In Brief

College is very different from high school; help your student navigate the differences up front—don't wait for the first challenge to crop up.

Help your student take charge of their education and become an active learner—that's required in college.

Don't assume that a strong student in high school automatically becomes a strong student in college. Help your student become a strong college student by using their college's resources.

References

1. *Digest of Education Statistics, 2018.* (2017). National Center for Education Statistics. https://nces.ed.gov/programs/digest/d18/tables/dt18_317.40.asp

2. Bowen, L. (2018, September 11). *State Funding: A piece of Temple's Tuition Puzzle.* Temple News. https://temple-news.com/state-funding-a-piece-of-temples-tuition-puzzle/

3. *Lawmaker Pushes Pennsylvania's State-Related Universities to Become More Transparent.* (2019, June 14). Nauman Smith. https://www.nssh.com/2019/06/lawmaker-pushes-pennsylvanias-state-related-universities-to-become-more-transparent/

4. Miller, M. (2018, September 12). *Average Cost of College in America: 2019 Report.* Value Penguin. https://www.valuepenguin.com/student-loans/average-cost-of-college

5. Turk, J. (2019, June 26). *Erasing the Community College Stigma*. Higher Education Today. https://www.higheredtoday.org/2019/06/26/erasing-community-college-stigma;/

6. Talley, F. J. (2020, March 12). *Community College Is Not the 13th Grade*. Helping Your College Student Succeed. http://www.collegeandparents.com/2020/03/12/community-college-is-not-the-13th-grade/

7. Murphy, S. (2015, May 12). *Mapping the Growing Importance of Student Affairs*. The EvoLLLution. https://evolllution.com/opinions/mapping-growing-importance-student-affairs/;

8. *About Student Affairs*. (2015). NASPA. https://www.naspa.org/about/about-student-affairs/about-student-affairs

9. *Six Things That Make College Teachers Successful*. (2018, July 9). Faculty Focus | Higher Ed Teaching & Learning. https://www.facultyfocus.com/articles/effective-teaching-strategies/six-things-make-college-teachers-successful/

10; *Quick Guide: Types of College Courses*. (n.d.). BigFuture. https://bigfuture.collegeboard.org/find-colleges/academic-life/quick-guide-types-of-college-courses

11. Talley, F. J. (2018, September 4). *The Syllabus*. Helping Your College Student Succeed. http://www.collegeandparents.com/2018/09/04/the-syllabus/

12. *Active Learning for the College Classroom*. (2013, October 23). Cal State LA. https://www.calstatela.edu/dept/chem/chem2/Active/main.htm

13. Bonswell, C. C., & Elson, J. A. (1991). *Active Learning: Creating Excitement in the Classroom. 1991 ASHE-ERIC Higher Education Reports*. ERIC Clearinghouse on Higher Education. Washington, DC: George Washington University.

14. Silvers, K. (2016, September). *Why General Education Classes Are More Important Than You Think*. Herzing University. https://www.herzing.edu/blog/why-general-education-classes-are-more-important-you-think;

15. Walden University. *Top Advantages of General Education Requirements in College*. (2019, January 28). Walden University. https://www.waldenu.edu/programs/resource/top-advantages-of-general-education-requirements-in-college

Chapter 3 - Majors and Minors

Family members of college students often them ask about their majors, which is why I'm addressing them here. In fact, everyone asks about them. Many ask this because they have an idea of the field students ought to go into because of the job market. They'll tell students to major in computer science when their passion is helping people, and they might be better suited to major in psychology or sociology. Students also talk about majors as soon as they arrive on campus. The first three questions they often hear are: (1) What's your name? (2) Where are you from? and (3) What's your major? Students who don't have an answer to the last question feel out of place in a heartbeat.

The pressure to choose a major and broadcast it to the world is incredibly high, and so is the pressure to choose a major that guarantees a good job after graduation. Students are also impatient to take courses in the major to the exclusion of their general education courses.[1] But before we get too far ahead, let's talk about what a major is and what it isn't.

A major is a related series of courses students take that focus their education.[2] Majors aren't the same as a career. A student graduating with a degree in mathematics may become a financial analyst or data analyst for an insurance company, or the psychology graduate may work on developing surveys for a marketing company. Majors provide students with specific tools they can apply to a variety of jobs, though they are often associated with a defined list of careers. It's unusual for chemistry majors to pursue careers in human resources, for example, because there isn't much connection between those two fields. They are far more likely to pursue careers that involve the sciences or scientific decision making. Majors that equate to careers are far more likely in the career programs offered by community colleges such as HVAC, plumbing, or nursing.[3] Also, keep in mind that students don't have to choose their major before they start college.

One of my students started college in 2015 and was very passionate about his psychology major, but he returned for his sophomore year saying he and his family worried about him getting a job after college. They had decided that he'd have more and better job opportunities as a computer science major. Seven years after he started college, this student had still not graduated, was at least three semesters from finishing, and struggled through much of the required coursework *because he probably shouldn't be a computer science major.* Choosing a major because there are jobs in that field is a red flag to me and my colleagues because that career may have little if any connection to the student's interests, abilities, or values. In fact, choosing a major is one of the last things students should do when thinking about going to college. Stay with me on this one.[4]

I believe students should first determine the general career or career area they'd like. They should think of things like whether they want to work outside or inside and whether they enjoy working with people or mostly alone. Maybe your student prefers problem solving whether people are involved or not. If they love the sciences or really hate the sciences, that should help them decide on potential careers as well. Afterward, the student can look online to find out how people in certain fields got there. They should also consider their values: what's important to them, and what impact do they want to have in the world? Considering all these factors should give them a general idea of a career field, or fields, they should pursue.

The next part of the process is to find out the kinds of courses that may lead to that career. A researcher into water quality needs courses in biology or ecology, for example, while someone who wants to work with youth should have a background in psychology or sociology. Students can identify patterns by looking at what people need to enter and flourish in a career. When that pattern looks very much like the requirements for a college major, that's the major they ought to choose. And for most students, that can be more than one choice.

Did you know a student can graduate as an art major yet still attend medical school? That's rare, but a student can complete art degree requirements while also taking the required pre-med courses in biology, chemistry, math, and physics and be qualified to enter medical school. In fact, entering law school students come from a wide number of undergraduate majors other than political science, the often go-to prelaw major.[5,6]

My point about taking the long view of choosing a major is this: if your student explores careers and finds something they want to pursue, they should work *backward* toward the major. That way, they can pursue that major with a passion they wouldn't have if they're thinking "this major leads to this career, and this career only" or "the only way to this career is with this major." What I'm suggesting is a longer process, and that's why career centers want students to visit their offices as early as possible so they can chart their path to a career using all the resources available to them.

The same applies to minors: they often emerge as students take courses that interest them or are seen as complimentary to their major.[7] Students frequently realize they were one course from completing a minor simply by taking courses they enjoyed. Other students—like me—use their minors to further focus the major into their proposed graduate degree field.

Two points as I finish: the major your student pursues may not make sense to you, or you might feel it gives them few or no career choices. That is unlikely to be the case. When I was in college and realized I would not cut it as a biology major, the only thing my father said to me was "and don't go changing it to sociology. There are sociology majors all over the place without a job." My father was a great guy, but after seeing what sociology courses are like and what sociology graduates can do at the end, he was dead wrong. If your student chooses a major that you question, ask them about their decision-making process, how they intend to use the major, and what career they want to pursue that aligns with the major. If they don't have the answers to those questions, suggest that finding them is important. Further, point them toward the resources at their college that can help them.

A second point is that most college students change their majors two or three times while in college—as I did—yet still graduate on time. What's important is for them to make informed choices about majors and minors along the way, using the resources their college offers.

Final point: most students only need a major and their general requirements to graduate.[7,8] Your student does not need two majors and two minors. This often leads to high and unnecessary stress. Suggest that they start slow with their major and discover other options along the way. You'll both sleep better for it.

In Brief

Encourage your student to choose their majors *after* considering the kind of career they might want. The career center is a great source of help for this decision.

A major isn't the same thing as a career, but it provides focus to their education and can help them chart a smooth path to their career.

The major—and their intended career—have to be a good fit for your student, not necessarily for your view of your student.

They don't need to have a minor, nor do they need to lock into a major before they start college.

If they change their major a time or two, don't fret. They should still be able to graduate on time.

References

1. Talley, F. J. (2018, July 13). *Why Is She Taking So Many Courses That Aren't in Her Major?* Helping Your College Student Succeed. http://www.collegeandparents.com/2018/07/13/why-is-she-taking-so-many-courses-that-arent-in-her-major/

2. Moody, J. (2018). *What a College Major Is and How It Can Shape Your Future.* US News & World Report. https://www.usnews.com/education/best-colleges/articles/2018-12-12/what-a-college-major-is-and-how-it-can-shape-your-future

3. Koenig, R. (2018). *Your College Major Does Not Define Your Career.* US News & World Report. https://money.usnews.com/careers/applying-for-a-job/articles/2018-09-24/your-college-major-does-not-define-your-career

4. Brush, K. (2016, October 21). *What No One Tells You about Deciding Late on a Major.* Student Caffé Blog. http://blog.studentcaffe.com/deciding-late-major/

5. *What Should I Major In If I Want to be a [Insert Impressive Job Title Here]?* (2016, May 9). College of St. Scholastica. http://www.css.edu/the-sentinel-blog/what-should-i-major-in.html

6. Eilers, C. (2018, January 15). *What Should I Major In? How to Choose a Major in 9 Steps.* Zety. https://zety.com/blog/how-to-choose-a-major

7. Wignall, A. (2022). *What Is a Minor in College and Should You Have One?* College Raptor. https://www.collegeraptor.com/find-colleges/articles/college-majors-minors/exactly-college-minor-minor-something/;

8. Talley, F. J. (2018, December 4). *Checking on Degree Progress.* Helping Your College Student Succeed. http://www.collegeandparents.com/2018/12/04/checking-on-degree-progress/

Chapter 4 - Choosing a College

Let's start from the beginning. When your student decides to attend college, they make a series of decisions, each one building on the previous one. First, ask your student why they want to attend college. This is not to discourage them but to learn what is motivating them to attend college. As a career educator, I'm happy they're making the choice to pursue education or training after high school.

Keep in mind that there are entire books written on how to choose a college, and there are many ways you can be involved as a parent (your student wants this, too, because of your influence in their life!)[1] Here is my take on the most important college choice suggestions or methods.

But before we get into that, let me address something parents often ask me: when should we start? There's no one definitive answer to that question, though collegelifetoday, a now defunct website, had a great timeline, which I'll adapt below. A shortcut I'll share is this: it's all right to discuss the idea of careers with a seventh grader, but I wouldn't ask them which colleges they want to attend. But waiting until December of the student's senior year in high school is too late. This is my adaptation of College Life Today's timeline:[2]

Sophomore Year

- Spend time with the guidance counselor and parents thinking about post-high school plans.

- Ask what they want to do with their life (as best as they can say now!)

- Take any standardized test preps available.

- Discuss with family what they see in their future.
- Ask people they know, such as teachers, pastors, and others, where they went to college.

Junior Year

Fall

- Generate an initial large list of potential colleges and universities (up to twenty).
- Take fall PSAT or ACT.
- Attend a college fair to learn about potential colleges.
- Check out the schedule of college visit days and schedule a visit for those schools that seem viable.

Winter

- Compile a list of people to ask for recommendations (teachers, etc.).
- Go on campus visits.

Spring

- Take the SAT or ACT or both.
- Narrow list of schools from twenty to only ten.

Senior Year

Fall and Winter

- Take the SAT or ACT or both.
- Conduct final campus visits.
- Complete the FAFSA (Free Application for Federal Student Aid), which opens in October, file as early as possible.

- Decide whether to apply early action or early decision for any of their target schools.

- Hone their list to the top five choices, and second five choices, hoping to apply only to the top five.

Spring

- Create a list of pluses and minuses of each school to make the final decision once acceptances come in.

- Don't downplay the value of additional campus visits to schools if they're on the fence.

A personal note: My daughter was on the fence between two schools, and her visit to her eventual university—including meeting with her department chair and a classroom visit—sealed the deal for her. There's a changed dynamic when you're visiting a school that has admitted you. It feels different, and you are seeing the school with new eyes—looking more for the fit and less to sell yourself.

Creating the Initial List of Potential Schools

With this timetable in mind, the next step is to move from the more than 4,200 colleges or universities in the United States to a more manageable number. With your student in the driver's seat, they should answer the following questions:

- How far away do they want to go?

- What do they plan to pursue as a major?

- What size school seems the best for them?

- What setting do they want to be in, meaning urban, rural, suburban, or small town? There is a world of difference between the feel of a small college in the middle of a small town versus that same college in a large city, or in the middle of an expansive farming community. Let your student tell you what they want, or what think they want.

- What kind of campus life do they want? Is it important that they have a major football team whose games they can attend, or is an extensive performing arts program more important?

- Will they live at home or on campus?

- Is the degree they're seeking offered only by certain types of schools, such as community colleges or specialized institutions?

These are the questions your student should use to sort through the thousands of college choices available to them.

Let's take an example. Say you live in Ohio, your student is happy to remain in the state, and they aren't picky about whether the school they attend is public or private. However, they want a college of between 12,000 and 15,000 students. That eliminates several of the private schools in Ohio and several public ones with enrollments larger than 15,000. This is fine: if these preferences make sense for your student, that reduces the number of choices they need to evaluate.

And how do they find out about things like enrollments, public or private classifications, and campus activities? There are several search engines available to your student: they've probably been using them already. Here are a few I've used. They can be found by placing "college search engines" into any web browser.

College Board Big Future (bigfuture.collegeboard.org)

Collegedata (collegedata.com)

College InSight (college-insight.org)

College Navigator (nces.ed.gov.collegenavigator)

College Raptor (collegeraptor.com)

College Scorecard (collegescorecard.ed.gov)

Cappex (cappex.com)

Naviance (naviance.com)

College Confidential
(collegeconfidential.com/schools/search)

Niche (niche.com/colleges/search/best-colleges/)

Unigo (unigo.com)

College Simply (collegesimply.com)

College XPress (collegexpress.com)

Peterson's (petersons.com/college-search.aspx)

I recommend using more than one search engine, since you may learn different things from different websites. As noted on the Road2College website: "No single college search website is one-size-fits-all, and none is all things for all students. Using several college search engines guarantees a broader picture of what one can expect from the college experience."[3] The more research the better, but don't overwhelm your student. If they're set on staying in Ohio, why consider schools in Missouri unless there's a specific need to do so, such as a unique major? To be honest, even having the field narrowed to Ohio colleges only is still *a lot* of colleges to look into.

Academics should be a significant driver in their research. If they don't have a major in mind yet—and most students either don't have one or may change their majors once enrolled—they should seek schools offering a variety of majors. And students who are undecided shouldn't attend schools focusing solely on aviation or business, for example, because if they choose a major that isn't within those areas, they will have to transfer. This is not a tragedy, but it can be a pain for them and for you.

Try this: using a college search engine, have your student put in the information they think is important, focusing on major, distance from home, and size of school first. When the results appear, they should explore the websites of the colleges and examine them thoroughly. Have them take thirty minutes on each and as they look, they should ask themselves:

- How would I describe the school based on the website alone?
- Does the description match what I want?

Have them examine the buildings and grounds and whatever they can see of the community outside the college or university, since they'll be spending time there, too. Watch any videos on the sites for other helpful information.

There are also sources other than search engines students can use. Their guidance counselor can be a great source of information, and they may know schools where your student will feel at home. Consider the schools they recommend.

The College Choice Funnel

Once your student has identified a number of schools—twenty is a common number—they'll need a way of reducing that number to ten or fewer—but shoot for ten. Now, your student should begin their deeper search. College fairs are a great resource at this stage. College fairs are trade fairs at which colleges gather in arenas or larger facilities and talk about what their colleges offer. These can be challenging to navigate, but they offer the best chance to make personal contact with a school. They're also a low-risk way to pick up printed materials and get valuable information. I live in rural southern Maryland, a region with two college fairs, one for two smaller counties and another in the largest one. Each fair includes more than a hundred colleges and universities. Colleges get a table with about six feet of space around it, and there's *a lot* of noise. Making the most of a college fair requires a plan. Find out which schools on your student's top twenty (or so) list will be at your local college fair and make a beeline for those schools.

At the fair, encourage your student to take the lead and ask questions, but avoid asking yes or no questions. Instead, have them ask questions such as:

- If I needed help in a course, what kind of support do you offer?
- What is the biggest selling point of your school?

- If we were to talk to a student at your college, what would they tell me about the faculty?

Use your imagination to brainstorm other questions with your student.

Also, make sure someone in your family attends sessions about financial aid and scholarships if they are offered. These are valuable and will help your student find scholarship resources in your home community.

When your student speaks with College A, they may discover the college doesn't have the major they want. This shouldn't happen often, since your student used their intended major as a search point, but sometimes they'll stop by a table because the college or university is well known in your region, or it's one you attended. But when your student asks about that major, listen to how the college representative responds. Many will say they don't offer that specific major but there are other majors that may help them toward their goal. If your student was interested in majoring in public policy, for example, a major in political science might fit their needs well. But be wary of schools suggesting that your student can design their own major. As noted in my "Work That College Fair" article, if your daughter really wants that school and wants to design a major, fair enough. The question to ask now is "how many students design their own majors in a year?" There's nothing wrong with a student-designed major. Many colleges and universities that allow student-designed majors have stringent rules on the process so the students will have a viable major. But many students are discouraged by the process itself and settle for another major that is second best in their mind. Don't be afraid to inject yourself here, since the decision on where to attend college is too important to leave to chance or a whim.[4]

Here's another tip: develop a separate email address for all college recruiting materials. Your student will receive a ton of materials, and the last thing you want is for your personal email or that of your student to be overwhelmed. Agree with your student that you'll all access the emails and discuss what comes in regularly.

On the way home, agree that unless they're just bursting with excitement about a particular school, you won't probe too heavily. Ask them to write a plus or minus for each school they've seen. You do the same thing, too, since that will provide additional perspective for your student.

And beyond the obvious features of setting and size, consider the climate of the school. When our daughter decided one of her top choices was Frostburg State—which is aptly named—I insisted we visit in the winter. During our campus tour, it began snowing. Yet because the school was still a suitable match for her, neither she, my wife, nor I felt the snow would be a problem. We had other neighbors whose middle daughter attended the University of Alabama. Her parents insisted she visit the campus during the summer so she could experience what it would be like during much of the year. She chose Alabama and graduated four years later, and she appreciated the experience of visiting during the summer.

Accreditation

Once your student has made tentative choices about which schools are in and which are out, the next step is to apply. But before doing so, check for accreditation. You don't want your student applying to colleges that aren't accredited. Accreditation is a process colleges and universities use to strengthen quality control and make sure the college education they are offering is worthy of the term. This ensures that when your student earns their degree, employers and graduate schools know they have completed an approved college education.

There are two important benefits of attending an accredited institution. First, the accreditation process ensures students are earning legitimate college credits at reputable institutions. This means that should your student transfer schools because the first college wasn't a good fit, their credits can transfer to another school. There is no guarantee every credit will transfer since some courses your student takes may not be offered by the second school, but at least they have a good chance of transferring. If your student earns credits from a nonaccredited school on the other hand, those credits most likely *won't* transfer.

The second benefit of accreditation is the fact that the federal government provides financial aid only to students attending accredited institutions. If your student attends a nonaccredited college, they are ineligible for federal financial aid, whether that aid be in the form of grants or loans.

The primary organizations that offer accreditation are approved by the Council for Higher Education Accreditation (CHEA). They're listed below and are known as the regional accrediting bodies. Many also accredit K-12 education.

>Accrediting Commission for Community and Junior Colleges (ACCJC)

>Western Association of Schools and Colleges (WASC)

>Higher Learning Commission (HLC)

>Middle States Commission on Higher Education (MSCHE)

>New England Commission of Higher Education (NECHE)

>Northwest Commission on Colleges and Universities (NWCCU)

>Southern Association of Colleges and Schools Commission on Colleges (SACSCOC)

>WASC Senior College and University Commission (WSCUC)[5]

Check first to see if the colleges your student is considering are regionally accredited: that's the usual gold standard. Other, faith-based schools might be accredited by the Transnational Association of Christian Schools and Colleges. Some of these schools also hold regional accreditation while others don't. Other accrediting bodies include the Association for Biblical Higher Education, Association of Advanced Rabbinical and Talmudic Schools, Association of Theological Schools, Commission on Accrediting, and Distance Education Accrediting Commission. Be sure to check for each school your student is interested in.

Another category of accreditation is for individual programs, such as one for business programs or one for nursing. While this type of accreditation isn't required for undergraduate programs, it identifies those programs deemed strongest by that accrediting body. There are some accreditations that you definitely want for your student's major. For example, I wouldn't enroll in an engineering program that wasn't accredited by (or at least a candidate for) the Accrediting Board for Engineering and Technology (ABET). Another important one for aspiring educators is the Council for the Accreditation of Educator Preparation (CAEP). As your student considers specific programs at colleges and universities, have them ask about accreditation of those programs. You can also find more information about accrediting bodies at the CHEA website, chea.org.

Once you're sure the college or university is accredited, but before you have your student rush into filling out either the institution-specific application or the common application, remember that, in my opinion, no student needs to apply to twenty colleges. Let's be honest: are they likely to attend all those schools? My personal philosophy is that your student should apply to five schools they would be happy attending, with a few schools beyond that if something goes wrong. Students shouldn't apply to a college or university they wouldn't be comfortable attending—at least in the early stages. Students often include their local community college on the list. That makes sense for several reasons. For one thing, they may not feel comfortable going away to school in the beginning, or perhaps they have family obligations and don't want to leave home yet. Students may also include their community college because they're undecided on their major and want to attend school locally to save money until they choose; then they'll invest in going away to school.

And even if their local community college isn't their first choice, keeping it on the list is a good idea. The same applies to colleges that are close enough for commuting. But keeping additional colleges on the list simply because they can, makes little sense to me. This is the dilemma of the common application.

Common Application Versus Institution-Specific Applications

The common application was first developed in 1975 so students could apply to many colleges at once. Students can complete the common app and send it to schools without looking through the requirements of each school's specific application. That's great and has made the process easier and less expensive for students. But it has also fueled an explosion of students applying to twenty or more schools.

As a former dean of enrollment management, I always appreciated students who completed our institution-specific application because it suggested they were particularly interested in our school. How can you know how serious a student is when they can apply to thirty colleges using a single application? The common app is an innovation that works well for students, but not so much for colleges. However, a student may do well to use the institution-specific application for their first-choice school to show that school how serious they are.

When to Apply

That's another question to explore: should your student apply to college early in the senior year (often by November 1) or during the regular admissions process (deadline of February 1 or so)? To answer this question, they need to consider what their early options are.

Early decision has been around for many years, and for the majority of schools with early decision, it's a binding agreement between the student and the college or university. If the student is admitted to the college, they agree to attend that school and withdraw applications from all the other schools they applied to. Sounds kinda restrictive, doesn't it? Well, it is. Colleges have early decision in place to help them build the entering class they want, and they often say that early decision applicants may receive preference for some scholarship aid over later applicants. One downside of early decision, however, is that students must commit to their schools in December or January, which is before final financial aid packages are sent out, so they're committing without knowing the final costs.

Another reason to apply early decision, according to The Princeton Review, is the fact that doing so shows the college how serious the student is. Schools may look more favorably on someone whose interest in their school is so high they're willing to forgo others to attend.⁶

Early action is non-binding, which means students can still apply to other schools, even once they are admitted to an early action school. My daughter applied early action to all three of her schools, so she knew what her options were as early as possible. An advantage of early action is that students still have until May 1 to decide where to attend and to pay their enrollment deposit. And since this is usually after they receive their financial aid award letter, early action applicants can consider their financial aid package as part of the college choice process.⁷

The advantages of early action to applicants are clear: they have the satisfaction of knowing they "got in," can compare financial aid packages, and don't have to make a final enrollment decision until May 1. Colleges that want to secure their entering classes as soon as they can prefer the early decision process, since they secure their class earlier. If early action doesn't obligate you to anything, and won't increase your cost, go for it, just be aware that once your student is admitted, they'll receive more information and contacts from that school hoping to convert them from an admitted student to a deposited/committed student.

Recommendation Letters

Earlier in this chapter, I included a list of tasks for the sophomore and junior years, including contacting people who can serve as references. When your student requests a recommendation, they should give the recommender the forms they need to write the recommendation, plus a personal statement from your student, or even a resume. Your student should give their recommenders as many tools as possible to write compelling letters. The best recommendations I've read (and I've read a few thousand!) are those that talk about specific things the student has done or that the recommender has observed. Once I know a recommender knows a student well, I give that recommendation much more weight than one that is non-specific and just "nice."

Interviews

Your student may also choose to interview with an admissions counselor. This is seldom required, but if your student believes they can make a positive impression and they want to visit the campus in that way, it's worth it. Your student should dress nicely and be prepared to speak about themselves and what they want to accomplish at the school. This is where good preparation comes in. I recommend they be prepared to speak about themselves with smiles on their faces (nervous or not) and to ask select questions about their proposed major, and so forth. Also, ask to visit a faculty member or the department chair for their proposed major.

Once They're Admitted

There are fewer more exciting moments than when a thick envelope arrives from one of your student's prospective colleges or universities, because you know a big envelope is part of the sales process. They're in! Now what? Now is the time to start a new phase of the process: making the final choice. I won't address finances in this chapter, but that should be part of the discussion. That financial conversation will focus on things such as out-of-pocket expenses, debt load per year, long-term debt, and so forth. But for now, let's think of the other intangibles about the schools.

I can't overemphasize the importance of the campus visit. Since you may have already toured the campus during a visit day, you don't need to do that again, although some colleges today will invite you specifically for admitted students as a way of converting your student. In that case, visit again! What I recommend is visiting the campus on a regular weekday when nothing specific is happening. That's the only way your student can be sure if the day-to-day vibe of the campus is what they want. This is challenging when a physical campus visit is impossible, such as during a health pandemic, for example. But that doesn't mean a campus visit-like experience can't be duplicated in other ways.

When you visit, have your student wear comfortable clothing, dressing how they think a college student might dress, casual, but not sloppy, and be prepared to look and listen. It really is all about the fit of your student at that school. A former Maryland legislator I know graduated from the University of Maryland, as did his wife and two older sons. So when his third and last son was considering universities, he visited the University of Maryland first, and liked it. Still, he followed through with a planned visit to Virginia Tech, and, according to my friend, the minute his son walked on campus, he said, "This is where I want to go to school." His son "knew" this was the school for him, and four years later, he had a degree from Virginia Tech and a big smile on his face.

I further recommend running the visit like this: have your student spend time with faculty in their intended major, visiting a class if possible, and go buy a cup of coffee in the campus snack bar. In fact, let your student do that and hang around to see how the other students interact. They will see in those instances how students normally act around each other. Have your student take mental note of which students say hello to them just because they're walking by, and which students are speaking with one another. While you're on campus, have at least someone in your family ask about tutoring services, or probe how students receive help in class or with personal issues. Explain to your student beforehand that while you don't expect them to fail, they'll want to know the resources that can support them should they need it. Make sure both you and your student check the website for this information as well.

In short, have them look carefully to decide if they can see themselves there, and ask them where on campus they felt the most comfortable. I hope they won't be able to identify a specific place, because nothing turned them off: they liked the department chair, they liked the class they visited, they bumped into a student who apologized and smiled at them. Further, they didn't see any students who appeared lonely or out of place. If they see many positives, and could see themselves thriving there, this may be "the one." Please allow your student to make this final call—with your input and guidance and with an eye toward the finances. But they're the ones who are going to be attending the school day in and day out, including when it's rainy and dreary and when they're stressed. If they say "yes" considering these things, you may have a winner!

In Brief

Students should start the process of looking at colleges beginning in their sophomore year of high school. Follow a plan.

Take the college search process step by step. And remember that with more than 4,200 colleges in the United States, your student shouldn't get hung up on "this college or nothing."

Major, size, and location are often the three most common features students search for while using college search engines.

College fairs are a great way to learn a little about a lot of colleges in one day.

Visit your students' preferred colleges if at all possible.

Consider applying early decision and early action if appropriate.

It's all about the fit: give your student the ability to make the final decision.

References

1. Workman, J. (1975). Review of *Parental Influence on Exploratory Students' College Choice, Major and Career Decision Making. College Student Journal, 49*(1).

2. *When to Apply to College Timeline.* (2020). Collegelifetoday.com. https://www.collegelifetoday.com/blog/tips/when-to-apply-college-timeline. Note: this link is currently inactive.

3. *Start with These College Search Websites.* (2019, August 1). Road2College. https://www.road2college.com/review-college-search-websites/

4. Talley, F. J. (2019, March 8). *Work that College Fair!* Helping Your College Student Succeed. http://www.collegeandparents.com/2019/03/08/work-that-college-fair/

5. *Regional Accrediting Organizations | Council for Higher Education Accreditation.* (2012). CHEA.org. https://www.chea.org/regional-accrediting-organizations

6. *Should You Apply Early Decision or Early Action?* (2020). Princeton Review. https://www.princetonreview.com/college-advice/early-action-vs-early-decision

7. Talley, F. J. (2019, April 20). *This College, That College: Which to Choose?* Helping Your College Student Succeed. http://www.collegeandparents.com/2019/04/20/how-to-choose-a-college/

Chapter 5 - Paying for College

How to pay for college is a challenging question for many families. Paying for college often requires sacrifice, planning, communication, and courage. College costs continue to rise, in good financial times and bad, and while there are "bargains" to be had, attending many colleges requires hard work by the student and their family.

First, let's differentiate between the cost of college and the price. Cost is what it costs the college or university to deliver the education your student receives. This includes items such as the salaries paid to employees, cost of maintaining facilities, materials, chemicals, food, and so forth. And yes, those costs have risen steadily for decades. The price of college is what the students pay to attend, and while that has risen steadily as well, keep in mind that what your student pays—even if they are paying with no outside financial help—*doesn't cover the full cost of their education*. Here's what I mean. Let's say your student attends a state college and the tuition, room, and board they have to pay is $20,000. However, if you look at the entire budget of the college and divide it by the number of students, you'll find that the cost of delivering that education to the student is actually $35,000. What makes up the difference? For state institutions, it's the state, but only to a degree. Colleges have other sources of funding, too, including foundation support, fundraising, grants the college receives, and so forth. So even when the college raises its price, the cost to the college of delivering that education to your student has gone up by at least as much. That's not a comforting thought when you're looking at a price tag though, is it? And that's why people seek financial assistance to attend college.

There are several basic types of financial aid or financial assistance. The first is gift aid in the form of scholarships or grants. These are not paid back. Grants are offered to students based on their financial need, and scholarships are usually awarded because of students' previous achievements or talents. For example, a student may receive a merit-based scholarship because of their sport talent or because of their high grades in school.[1] And speaking of the family, this is important to know: governments and organizations approach financial assistance with the view that the primary source of funding for a student's education is their family. This is important because even with all the government-sponsored sources of money out there, the first place students should look for funds is their family. The government steps in only to fill any gaps that may exist.[2, 3]

And if you think you shouldn't even bother to apply for financial aid because of your higher income, keep this in mind from Michelle Singeltary from her syndicated column "The Color of Money":

> "Lots of state aid programs ask that you file the FAFSA—the Free Application for Federal Student Aid as well. Even colleges and universities which offer merit aid want the FAFSA information on file to see if there are special programs your student might qualify for that have little to do with financial need. And since filing the FAFSA is free, filing it should be a no-brainer."[4]

Also, keep in mind that the federal financial aid formula considers the number of students in a family who are enrolled in college at the same time. So when two students in a family are enrolled in college as opposed to just one, both students may be eligible for aid, even when the single student wasn't eligible before.[5]

Loans and work study are known as self-help sources of funding. Loans are paid back, and I'll address those later. Students who are eligible for work study will receive that as part of their financial aid award letter. This means they are eligible to work an on-campus job to give them pocket money. And the only way your student can gain access to these funds is by completing the FAFSA.[2,5]

The FAFSA

I'm sure you've heard horror stories about how difficult the FAFSA is to complete. I'd say it's challenging, but no more difficult than filing your taxes with an additional schedule or two. But regardless of your experience with your taxes, the FAFSA is intimidating. Gird yourself for this battle, because you need to navigate this with your student so they can access the financial aid available to them, even those that may be merit based. While filling it out, you'll think you're revealing everything about your financial past, and that's true. Just go with it and understand that every parent filling out the FAFSA feels the same way: it's a necessary evil. An excellent source for information on federal forms of aid is student.gov. Check it out.

Colleges and libraries in your area may provide free assistance to help you complete the FAFSA. These are excellent sources, too, both for how to pay for college and for information about colleges in your area. Don't forget them.

When you file the FAFSA, the system determines what they call your financial need, called the Expected Family Contribution (EFC). This is a figure that the method says your family should be able to pay for your student to attend college. When you're looking at a particular college's price, that college provides their cost of attendance (COA), which is what it takes to pay for tuition, housing, meals, fees, transportation, and other expenses. Subtracting the EFC from the COA tells you how much your student is eligible for in terms of financial assistance, but it doesn't mean that your student automatically qualifies for that much aid.

Once your student has been accepted to a college and has applied for financial aid, they'll receive an award letter. This award letter tells you the college's cost of attendance and the aid they can receive at that college. The bottom line—after all aid is awarded to your student—is what the student has to pay out-of-pocket for that year. If you or your student take out a loan, you'll need to factor in the eventual payments for those as well. Speak with your student about debt load, and make sure you're all comfortable with the amount of debt the student may graduate with.[6]

Here's an example from the collegeandparents.com blog that explains how to use the award letter and other information to decide where to attend:

	Whole Grain State College	Independent University
Tuition	$12,000	$35,000
Housing	$4,500	$9,200
Meals (19/week)	$5,500	$6,300
Mandatory fees	$500	$1,100
Personal expense, including transportation	$2,500	$2,500
Total	$25,000	$54,100

On the face of it, Whole Grain is the clear winner, at least in terms of price. But let's dig a little deeper. Student A has an EFC of $3,200 per year.

	Whole Grain Cost of Attendance	Independent University Cost of Attendance
Total Cost	$2,500	$54,100
EFC	$3,200	$3,200
Financial Aid Eligibility	$21,800	$50,900

Student A is eligible for much more financial aid at Independent University than at Whole Grain. But what about merit awards from colleges and universities? These grants may come from the college's endowments or operating budgets. Let's change Student A's equations adding merit awards to both calculations.

	Whole Grain Cost of Attendance	Independent University Cost of Attendance
Total Cost	$2,500	$54,100
EFC	$3,200	$3,200
Merit Awards	$3,000	$24,000
Financial Aid Eligibility	$18,800	$26,900

Keep in mind that these figures don't include any state grants that Student A might be eligible for. As you can see, the gap between the financial aid eligibility for the two schools narrows with the addition of the merit award figures.[7]

Another thing you should examine are outside scholarships.[8] Two places to look for them are a top ten list from US News and careeronestop.org, which is compiled by the US Department of Labor.[9] Have your student check them out to see what they can apply for. Also, ask the financial aid offices of any potential schools about how that school counts outside financial aid in their aid package. Chances are they will count those dollars as part of the student's aid package and may reduce what they're willing to provide if your student receives lots of outside aid.[10] This is a disincentive for seeking those scholarships and going through the application process, but most schools do that so their financial aid dollars can help more students. If your student finds a financial aid source that will pay money to them directly or provide them with things like books or other equipment, that's a real winner.

Another way of paying for college is to determine what your family can afford on a monthly basis and pay for at least some costs that way. That's what my parents did many years ago and how we covered our daughter's funding gap for three of her four years of college. (We took out a loan for her first year thinking we might get too stressed out with the payment plan.) Payment plans are great because, like a loan, they allow you to pay over time, and while that puts a crimp in your other spending, handling that over eight to ten months was much easier than paying large chunks twice a year. We also avoided the finance charges and interest associated with a loan. Check out your student's preferred colleges to find out how they structure their payment plans. Lots of schools have them, and they are a great way to pay for college.[11]

Don't forget to look at your state's sources of funding as well. This site—collegescholarships.org—shows you where to go in your state for information and how to apply for state assistance. These funds may be available to your student even if they attend a college out of state.[8]

To summarize:

1. Don't choose a college solely based on the tuition

2. Always file the FAFSA, even if you think you aren't eligible or you weren't eligible the year before

3. Talk openly about finances

4. Involve your student from day one[7,12]

In Brief

Cost isn't the same as price when it comes to paying for college, but that may not make any difference to you.

Basic types of financial aid are grants, loans, and work study.

Always file the FAFSA—even if your student didn't qualify before, or you believe you're too wealthy. Your student's school may require the FAFSA for non-need-based scholarships.

The FAFSA can be intimidating, but look for help in your community to complete it.

Always look at the "bottom lines" when you see a financial aid offer—including both the out-of-pocket costs and the kind of debt your student will graduate with—before making a final decision.

References

1. Farrington, R. (2019, January 25). *How to Find Grants to Pay for College.* The College Investor. https://thecollegeinvestor.com/21220/find-grants-pay-college/

2. Powell, Farran. (2014). *An Ultimate Guide to Understanding Financial Aid for College.* US News & World Report. https://www.usnews.com/education/best-colleges/paying-for-college/articles/an-ultimate-guide-to-understanding-college-financial-aid;

3. *Types of Financial Aid.* (2019, July 5). Federal Student Aid. https://studentaid.gov/understand-aid/types

4. Talley, F. J. (2018, October 4). *Yes, You Can Apply for Financial Aid.* Helping Your College Student Succeed. http://www.collegeandparents.com/2018/10/04/applying-for-financial-aid/

5. *How Siblings Affect Financial Aid Packages | College Coach Blog.* (2020, April 23). The Insider: Your Expert Guide to College Admissions. https://blog.getintocollege.com/financial-aid-the-sibling-factor/

6. Talley, *Yes, You Can Apply.*

7. Talley, F. J. (2018, July 6). *FAFSA 101 or, a Primer on Financial Aid*. Helping Your College Student Succeed. http://www.collegeandparents.com/2018/07/06/fafsa-101-or-a-primer-on-financial-aid/

8. Talley, F. J. (2019, August 23). *Applying for Outside Scholarships*. Helping Your College Student Succeed. http://www.collegeandparents.com/2019/08/23/applying-for-outside-scholarships-and-they-impact-a-students-financial-aid-package/

9. Soriano, Deborah Ziff. (2017). *10 Sites to Kick Off Your Scholarship Search*. US News & World Report. https://www.usnews.com/education/best-colleges/paying-for-college/articles/2017-09-14/10-sites-to-kick-off-your-scholarship-search; *CareerOneStop Scholarship Finder*. (2020). Careeronestop.org. https://www.careeronestop.org/Toolkit/Training/find-scholarships.aspx

10. *Federal Student Aid—IFAP: Search Results*. (n.d.). Ifap.ed.gov. https://ifap.ed.gov/search?keywords=outside+scholarship+policies

11. Talley, F. J. (2019, January 8). *Payment Plans—Another Way to Pay*. Helping Your College Student Succeed. http://www.collegeandparents.com/2019/01/08/payment-plans-another-way-to-pay-for-college/

12. *Find State Grants for College Students*. (n.d.). Collegescholarships.org. http://www.collegescholarships.org/grants/state.htm

Chapter 6 - The Decision

So, your student has finally decided on the college they want to attend. Hooray! They've weighed the major, location, size, finances, and fit and are sure this is the best choice. If this wasn't your student's first choice or dream school, don't fret. The fact is, the school they attend may not mean much ten years later. Sure, there are schools such as those in the Ivy League that will always have an aura surrounding them, but most employers looking for new employees want to know if the person has a degree, not whether that degree is from Palmdale Polytech or Western State College: having the degree is what matters. Note: a close colleague of mine implores students *not* to switch to their second-choice colleges if possible. Her suggestion is to attend a community college, then try to transfer into the dream school after receiving an associate degree. It's a method that's worth considering.

Enrollment Deposits

Your student's next step is paying the enrollment deposit. This is often a few hundred dollars and secures your student's spot in the incoming class. For most four-year institutions, the common candidate reply date is May 1. That has changed in recent years, and with the pandemic shifting norms, many colleges and universities accept enrollment deposits after that date. However, keep in mind that your student may have fewer academic options if they don't deposit on time. The same may be true for housing options. If your student is sure about their school earlier than May 1, such as mid-March, send in your enrollment deposit then. This will reduce the number of conversion emails they receive from their school of choice (or the ones they *didn't* chose) and will increase the emails and other communications about things like finding a roommate, orientation, and so forth, from their school of choice. Another thing: your student isn't required to tell schools when they won't be attending; however, telling them they're no longer interested lets them off the hook and they won't have to endure countless emails, texts, and phone calls from them, so it's a win-win.[1]

For some families, paying the enrollment deposit is a financial hardship. Be sure to ask your admissions counselor if the deposit may be waived. Also, the enrollment deposit is often non-refundable but may be applied to the overall tuition bill.

Once they pay the deposit, they're in! Now, encourage your student to buy what we call "swag"—items of clothing from their intended college to show their friends and neighbors where they're going to school. Expect that the tone or content of messages from their college will change from "we want you" to "here's the next step." Pay close attention to all of the incoming communications from the institution. I recommend holding a regular weekly or twice per week discussion with your student on the status of tasks to be completed before enrollment. Pay close attention to things such as spring orientation dates, summer orientation, forms that have to be completed (health, etc.) or placement tests your student has to take online before school begins in the fall. Their college may hold spring orientation in June, which often consists of a one-day session on campus with groups of incoming students. Please attend because this program is designed more for you than for your student. I'm referring to it as spring orientation to distinguish it from the orientation that occurs just before classes begin in August or September.[2]

Spring Orientation

Think about this: traditional-aged students—those between eighteen and twenty-two—are caught up in the euphoria of graduating from high school, and they are not yet focused on the year ahead. You, on the other hand, are worried about the roommate they'll have, whether they'll make friends, how they'll handle their new freedom, and how you're going to pay the bill. Colleges and universities know this, and they hold parent orientation sessions so you can learn how to support your student. In fact, during spring orientation, parents and family members ask far more questions than their students do.

During spring orientation, both you and your student may attend a variety of sessions on what to expect for the coming year, and at some point, colleges often separate students from their parents for placement tests or for academic advising as they plan their first-term schedule. I know you want to be there with them, but academic advisors are trained to help students choose the right courses to get them on their way. Trust them and your student to make the right choices, and even if your student isn't able to take a course in their major during the first term, they have plenty of time to make that up, since students take around 40 percent of their courses outside of their major during their undergraduate coursework. (Please encourage your student to lobby for at least one course in their major anyway!) They also need to learn early on to take the lead in advising opportunities and in registering for their courses. Talk to them before and after their advising appointment. The collegeandparents.com blog has plenty of information on advising appointments that you can read at your leisure.[3]

Finding a Roommate

Another important task for entering students who will live on campus is choosing a roommate. Finding or being matched with a roommate has changed quite a bit during the last ten years due to social media, but there are several ways your student can find a roommate. First, keep in mind that they don't have to room with their best friend, and probably shouldn't.[2, 4] Nor will their assigned roommate necessarily become their best friend. More on that later. The oldest method of roommate assignments was for students to complete a survey asking them things such as sleeping habits, music taste, and preference on visitors. Based on the result of the survey, colleges assigned students who were basically compatible. These pairings were not perfect, but with the proper support, the pairing could work fine for a year. My daughter's first roommate "kind of" worked for her, but only for a year. But from that first-year experience, my daughter learned excellent negotiating skills, which served her as a Resident Assistant for the following three years. And while I thought the survey method worked well, my daughter and others don't favor it, and this stemmed from how well they matched with their first roommates. Use these surveys with your eyes open, but ask students (or the parents of students) who already attend your student's preferred school how they found their roommates.

Newer methods include students using social media to find their roommates. This method can work well, but it doesn't force the students to explore deeper issues about roommate expectations. An additional method is for students to be assigned as part of a living learning community. These communities often follow themes such as environmental activism or substance-free housing and give the students strong connections with sponsoring faculty or staff at their college.[5]

One thing I recommend against is requesting a roommate during spring orientation, especially if that program involves an overnight stay. Students come to these programs full of anxiety and worried about who they'll meet. So when they meet a nice person during that program, they latch on to that person like a barnacle, declaring that they want to live with them. These pairings seldom succeed since neither student has really thought the decision through: they just found someone who wasn't an axe murderer and latched on to them. Discourage your student from doing this.[6]

Once they have a roommate, your student should speak with them before school to discuss things such as who is bringing a refrigerator or other devices and how they wish to decorate the room. In short, have them start a dialogue with their roommate so they get off on the right foot. A successful roommate relationship does not happen without work.

The Summer Before College Transition

Now, you have a couple of months to enjoy family activities with your student before your family dynamic changes. Don't be shy about asking your student to participate in a family vacation or visit relatives they haven't seen for a while. Recognize, though, that your student will want to spend similar time with their friends who are also going away to college. Work on communication with your student now since that will serve you when they leave. This is important since your relationship with your student and their educational institution will change forever once they start college.

Keep in mind that the summer before college is a good time to open lines of communication between you and your student. The Family Educational Rights and Privacy Act (formerly called the Buckley Amendment) was passed in 1974 and specifies that once students reach the age of eighteen—or begin college—they are legally adults.[5,7] This also means that their educational records belong to them and not to their parents. Yes, you are (often) paying the bills, but your student is in control. If you want to know what's happening with your student on campus, your primary source is speaking with them. Work on building those lines of communication now.[8]

Also, discuss spending guidelines as they prepare for college. What do you expect them to spend for snacks or pizza during the week? How flexible can that be, and when will you decide not to replenish their debit card if you see excessive spending? While you don't want your student to starve or not participate with their new friends, they need to know that there are limits.[7,9] Having these discussions now, even when you have a temporary disagreement, will make the school year much smoother. And for those students living at home, don't expect because they're living there that things can or should stay the same. They should be on campus far more than their class schedule suggests. That way they can participate in college activities, study on campus, access the library, and meet with their advisor or faculty members. Understanding those expectations and requirements on both your parts will make the next few months easier as you prepare for their (your) transition to college.

In Brief

Be sure to pay your student's enrollment deposit by the required date—usually May 1.

There is still work to be done after sending in the enrollment deposit. Pay attention to emails and other communications so your student doesn't forget something.

Attend spring orientation if your student's school sponsors one. It's worth it.

Help your student find a roommate—which probably shouldn't be their best friend. Ask upperclass students you know for their suggestions on how to find a roommate.

Discuss spending guidelines before college starts so you're on the same page.

References

1. Talley, F. J. (2019, November 20). *Early Decision and Early Action*. Helping Your College Student Succeed. http://www.collegeandparents.com/2019/11/20/early-decision-and-early-action/

2. Talley, F. J. (2019, June 25). *Spring Orientation*. Helping Your College Student Succeed. http://www.collegeandparents.com/2019/06/25/making-the-most-of-spring-orientation/

3. Talley, F. J. (2018, October 21). *What Academic Advising Is Supposed to Mean*. Helping Your College Student Succeed. http://www.collegeandparents.com/2018/10/21/whats-academic-advising/

4. Talley, *Spring Orientation*; Talley, F. J. (2019, July 10). *Roommates*. Helping Your College Student Succeed. http://www.collegeandparents.com/2019/07/10/roommates-in-college/

5. Talley, *Roommates*.

6. Talley, *Spring Orientation*.

7. *Parents' Guide to the Family Educational Rights and Privacy Act: Rights Regarding Children's Education Records—FPCO*. (2015). Ed.gov. https://doi.org/http://www.ed.gov/policy/gen/guid/fpco/brochures/parents.html

8. Talley, F. J. (2018, July 27). *Work on Communication Before School Starts*. Helping Your College Student Succeed.

http://www.collegeandparents.com/2018/07/27/effective-communication-with-your-college-student/

9. Talley, F. J. (2020, June 24). *Planning a Budget for Your College Student.* Helping Your College Student Succeed. http://www.collegeandparents.com/2020/06/24/planning-a-budget-for-your-college-student/

Chapter 7 - Transitioning to College

Here's a little understood secret: this transition is not just for your student, it's for you, too. Don't forget that or belittle it. Your student will go through several changes over the next few months, and so will you, in terms of family dynamics, finances, and so forth. These can be as significant for you as a family member as they are for your student.

For those of you whose students have gone away to college, please discourage them from coming home for at least six weeks.[1] Of course, for important family events, such as a wedding, you can ignore this rule. But in most cases, your student should stay on campus for those first six weeks. We've learned through long-standing research that most students decide to drop out of college *within the first six weeks of their first term in college.* This often occurs because the students aren't connected to their college and, therefore, aren't invested enough to stay. This happens more often if they go home every weekend. Bite the bullet and tell them they can't come home, and you can't pick them up. Discuss that during the summer so your expectation is clear.

I can't stress the importance of communication with your student. Do you expect them to call you every day (don't do that) or do you want occasional texts and a weekly or twice-a-week phone call? This latter is far more reasonable. Remember, your student could be all wrapped up in their activities and only remember about the daily phone call at 11:30 at night. Do you really want their call then? And the fact that they are so engaged in campus academics and other activities for so long every evening is a good thing and should be encouraged! Talk honestly about your expectations for communication, keeping in mind that the center of their universe just shifted to another location.[2] And if you need an excuse to connect with your student, take my wife's advice: take a selfie with friends or former teachers you see around town and send it to your student. That's sure to get them talking to you!

What to Bring to College

I have several blog posts on what to bring and not bring to college. Most students find they get along with far less than they planned. Our daughter took a lot of stuff (I mean, *a lot* of stuff) and while she used most of it, her roommate came with much less and got along fine. However, our daughter attended a college four hours away, while her roommate lived less than an hour from campus. It was no big deal for her roommate's dad to bring stuff to campus whenever he worked in the area; our daughter didn't have that option.[3,4]

High School to College

One of the biggest challenges for new students in college is understanding the differences between high school and college. I'll speak more about this in a later chapter, but one of the biggest shocks they experience is the amount of time they have to spend studying outside of class.[5] High school students are often given worksheets to complete in class or to guide their reading at home. In addition, high school classes might meet 180 hours over the course of the year to cover a subject. A college class meets between 45 and 60 hours to cover the same materials, and the college student has to learn it at a much deeper level.[6,7] What happened to the missing 120 to 135 hours? They're not lost; they're the hours your student spends outside of class learning the material. So, your student's out-of-class workload will rise significantly in college as compared to high school. We suggest students spend two to two-and-a-half hours outside of class for every hour they're in class. Most first-year students balk at this, but upperclass students—when they count everything academic that they do regularly—agree that it's accurate. Help your student get started with that by encouraging them to create a schedule of study times connected to their academic schedule. I suggest an agenda book as a great way to keep track of assignments. Many students say they just use their phones, which is a fine way of getting reminders. But having a copy in a written planner or agenda book is an even better tool, and many students agree.

Faculty Matters

Another significant difference between high school and college is the importance of working positively with college faculty from day one. This means students should visit each of their faculty members in their offices to introduce themselves. This is not sucking up to the professor, but a survival tactic. When a faculty member knows a student cares about their course, and their interactions with faculty are positive and respectful and show initiative, that professor is likely to give them the benefit of the doubt. [8,9]

And if your student has a class in their major during their first term in school, encourage them to meet with that faculty member in their office to discuss the major. This reflects their investment and also means when that faculty member is asked about students to suggest for a department activity, they will remember your student's name.[8] Faculty members *love* spending time with motivated students in their majors.

Relationship Changes

Your relationship with your student will change once they're in college, too. This is the case whether your student is living at home while attending college or living on campus. They will be in charge of everything they experience in college, including when to go to bed and when to get up, how long to study, what people to spend time with, when and how much to eat, and how to spend time outside of class. You've regulated these decisions for their entire lives, and while you'll be able to influence them now, ultimately, they will decide what they'll do and what they won't do. Please work on open communication long before your student starts college.

Theorists have long studied the changes college students experience while enrolled. Years ago, Arthur Chickering coined seven "vectors" of development. Clark University summarized Chickering's work so well, I've included it verbatim here. Take a look at this simple description of the seven vectors:

(1) Developing Competence

Although intellectual competence is of primary importance in college, this vector includes physical and interpersonal competence as well. The student who attends college seeking only credentials for entry into the work world is sometimes surprised to find that his or her intellectual interests and valued friendships change as a result of their personal development through the college years.

(2) Managing Emotions

Moving from adolescence to adulthood means learning how to manage emotions like anger and sexual desire. The young person who attempts to control these emotions by "stuffing" them finds they can emerge with more force at a later time.

(3) Developing Autonomy

Being able to take care of oneself, both emotionally and practically, is critically important to growing up and becoming independent from one's family of origin.

(4) Establishing Identity

The age-old question—who am I?—is asked and answered many times during a lifetime. Yet, that question has exquisite urgency and poignancy during the college years. This vector is especially problematic for women and ethnic minorities who may feel invisible in our society or have multiple roles to play in different situations.

(5) Freeing Interpersonal Relationships

First, one moves from valuing relationships based on need (dependence) to valuing individual differences in people. Next, the person learns how to negotiate those differences in relationships. Finally, the young person begins to understand the need for interdependence and seeks mutual benefit from relationships.

(6) Developing Purpose

The young person identifies her or his career and life goals and, hopefully, makes appropriate choices to achieve those goals.

(7) Establishing Integrity

This level of maturity does not come easily. Once achieved, however, the young adult is able to live with those uncertainties that exist in the adult world. In addition, he or she adapts society's rules so they become personally meaningful (Chickering, 1969).[10]

Another theorist I like is Nevitt Sanford. He identified the challenge and support mantra. Sanford said that for students to grow, they need to be challenged to take on ever more difficult tasks and expectations and be supported in their efforts to reach the new goals.[11] When your student calls you, complaining about a difficult class, that may be because the faculty member is ramping up the challenge and your student wasn't prepared for that. However, colleges have supports in place to help your student, starting with the faculty members themselves.[11]

Expect that you will become more of a consultant with your student.[12] If you have a good relationship with your parents now, think about how it was when you were younger. Your dad doesn't expect you to do everything he tells you to do now. If you call and ask for advice, you consider it, weigh it, and then decide what to do. That's what will happen with your student now. They will decide what to do after consulting with you. The consulting role is tougher for parents because we're often certain that the decision the student is considering is all wrong, and we know they'll fall on their faces. But this may be a time when they need to fall on their faces in order to grow as young adults. Seeing that temporary failure is one of the toughest things you will ever do.

Changes at Home

What about other parts of your transition? When you go home and see an empty room or bed while your student is away at college, you'll feel the difference. That's another reason you get teary-eyed when you get home after dropping them off, but push past this. As you focus differently on the student you've sent off to school, this can be an opportunity for you to develop a renewed focus on your other kids if you have them. Just be aware that sometimes you'll turn to tell your new college student something and they won't be at their usual spot at the table. This is also a great time to contact the parents of other new college students to commiserate with them. That will surely help with your transition.[2]

Community on Campus

As for your student, they have to find ways to "fit in." Most will live on a residence hall floor: that's one of their communities. Another community is the entire residence hall itself. Most residence halls for first-year students feature double rooms with perhaps a ratio of twenty students to each undergraduate resident assistant, or RA. That ratio provides mentorship to a smaller group of students, and the RA is charged with helping to build community on their floor as students adjust to campus. Encourage your student to make friends with their RA, and if they don't seem to get along, there are always other RAs in their building who may be willing to serve as an informal mentor for them.[13]

Every college and university sponsors campus activities, including dances, game nights, open mic nights, movies, or recreational tournaments. Encourage your student to attend these events during their first term in college, including finding a club they'd like to join. Their connection to the college doesn't occur only in the classroom: it happens in every area of the campus where they can become part of something bigger than themselves and find people who will care about them and their college journey.[13]

Students may also develop community with the people they see every day in the cafeteria—stay with me on this one. If they head to the cafeteria about the same time every Tuesday or another day, they are likely to see the same people. Suggest that they sit in a place they haven't before or strike up a simple conversation in the lunch line asking about or commenting on a particular item of food. That conversation may be the beginning of a friendship. This is one more way of connecting with other students. And as difficult as it may be for your student in the beginning, it gets much easier over time, and eventually they will be the ones encouraging shyer students to do the same. So if you're wondering if your student will make friends in college, the answer 99.9% of the time is "yes."

Another transition point is managing money. Your student may work an on-campus job or an off-campus job while in college—a great way to earn spending money. Jobs on campus are preferred for students, since those employers know that a student's first priority is their academics, not their job. If your student has worked for two years at a convenience store in your hometown, however, and can transfer for eight hours a week to a store nearby, that's a great way to get off campus, learn more about the town, and make money.[14] Before they leave for school, help them think about how they will spend money. What they learn about budget and finance as a younger adult will serve them well as they grow into later adulthood.

There are lots of transitions students go through during their first term in college. You'll go through many as well. Two goals of this book are to give you the tools to support your student through their transition and to help you through yours as well. And the best is yet to come.

In Brief

Discuss communication expectations before your student goes to college.

Your student doesn't need to bring everything to college if they aren't too far from home. Communicate with roommates on shared items such as refrigerators.

Remember how different college is from high school and help your student understand that, too.

Encourage your student to connect with their faculty as soon as possible.

Your student will grow in many ways while in college, not just intellectually.

Urge your student to become involved on campus to help with their transition and to make their college feel like a new home.

References

1. Talley, F. J. (2018, September 18). *Parent and Family Weekend: Do You Go?* Helping Your College Student Succeed. http://www.collegeandparents.com/2018/09/18/parent-and-family-weekend/

2. Harke, B. (2013, August 15). *New College Parents: Lost in the Transition.* HuffPost. https://www.huffpost.com/entry/new-college-parents-lost-_b_3751621

3. Talley, F. J. (2018, August 20). *What to Pack and What to Keep Home.* Helping Your College Student Succeed. http://www.collegeandparents.com/2018/08/20/what-to-pack-and-what-to-keep-home/;

4. Talley, F. J. (2019, August 12). *What to Bring, and What Not to Bring to College.* Helping Your College Student Succeed. http://www.collegeandparents.com/2019/08/12/what-to-bring-and-what-not-to-bring-to-college/

5. Weber, J. (2005). Review of *Parenting Your College Freshman.* Campus Life.

6. Talley, F. J. (2019, February 18). *Taking Control of Their Time as College Students.* Helping Your College Student Succeed. http://www.collegeandparents.com/2019/02/18/taking-control-of-their-time-as-new-college-students/;

7. Donham, J., & Rehmke, D. (2016). Review of *High School to College Transition: Sharing Research With Teachers*. Teacher Librarian, *44*(2), 13–17.

8. Talley, F. J. (2019, May 13). *Talking To College Faculty Members*. Helping Your College Student Succeed. http://www.collegeandparents.com/2019/05/13/talking-to-college-faculty-members/

9. Talley, F. J. (2018, July 27). *Work on Communication Before School Starts*. https://www.collegeandparents.com/2018/07/27/effective-communication-with-your-college-student/ Helping Your College Student Succeed.

10. https://web.archive.org/web/20101023075614/https://www.cabrini.edu/communications/ProfDev/cardevChickering.html, 2021.

11. Ward, K., Trautvetter, L., & Braskamp, L. (2005). Review of *Putting Students First: Creating a Climate of Support and Challenge*. Journal of College and Character, *VI*(8), 1–6.

12. Talley, F. J. (2018, July 8). *Becoming a Consultant to Your Student*. https://www.collegeandparents.com/2018/07/08/becoming-a-consultant-to-your-student/ Helping Your College Student Succeed.

13. Ruhl, K. (n.d.). *Finding Community on Campus*. https://www.collegiateparent.com/student-life/finding-community-on-campus/ Collegiate Parent.

14. Talley, F. J. (2020, June 24). *Planning a Budget for Your College Student*. Helping Your College Student Succeed. http://www.collegeandparents.com/2020/06/24/planning-a-budget-for-your-college-student/

Chapter 8 - Living Away from Home

If your student plans to live somewhere other than your home during college, they have two major options: living in college- or university-sponsored housing or living off campus in an apartment or shared house.

Living on Campus

Campus residences are generally referred to as residence halls, not dormitories, because residence halls are living learning programs as well as buildings.[1] Master's level professionals who are trained to provide low-level counseling, support, and encouragement to students often supervise these buildings. They also develop educational and social activities for your students through their undergraduate RA staff. In short, the residence halls are a professional learning environment like classrooms and laboratories.

Remind your student that their roommate may not be their best friend: they are simply a roommate. But even that can be difficult if your student has their own room at home. As your student leaves for campus, encourage them to think of what's important to them and to prepare themselves for less privacy than they have at home.

A way that colleges encourage roommates to negotiate is by urging them to develop a roommate contract.[2] This contract outlines their expectations for how the room is to be used, including things such as waking and working hours; what acceptable noise levels might be; who may sleep over; and so forth. Once students sign this document, it is a "contract" between the two roommates that they can consult for guidance when something goes wrong. The problem is this: say your student doesn't want any overnight visits of the opposite sex in their room even if that's allowed by their college. Does your student want to be "that student" who doesn't allow that in their room when all the other students allow it? Take another example. Your student is the same general size as their roommate, and the roommate likes your student's sweaters. Your student may not want to share clothes for whatever reason but feels that if they refuse, they won't be accepted. Most roommates aren't like this, but fear of a negative reaction may drive your student to be more accommodating in the roommate contract than they want to be.

Encourage your student to ask their RA to help with the contract. The RA can walk the roommates through several scenarios to help them. They may also see your student's (or their roommate's) discomfort with particular items in the contract and suggest ways to make the contract acceptable for all.

Other items in the roommate contract include things like who cleans what and how often and general hygiene expectations. And while preparing your student for college, get them in the habit of making their bed and doing their own laundry. They may not worry about making their bed at home, but that's their whole "house" in college, and they'll be spending more time in it than they do at home. A messy room makes studying more difficult by being distracting. And if they've never done laundry before, now is the time to learn.[3]

As mentioned earlier in this chapter, an important element of residence halls is programming offered by the RA staff under the supervision of the professional staff. This programming often follows the SPICES acronym (social, physical, intellectual, cultural, emotional, and spiritual) so that programming is balanced. In the beginning, more activities will be social so students can meet each other. As the term continues, other programs—such as how to prepare for the first academic advising meetings or how to choose a major—will be offered. Urge your student to attend these programs. They're a great way to meet students outside of their floor and connect with the RA, which may come in handy if they need help later.[4]

Lastly, encourage them to meet other students. Some students they meet on the first day of school will become friends for life, and why wait for that to happen? My daughter met a young woman at June orientation and was thrilled to see her living on her floor during her first year. She has since attended birthday parties and baby showers with this young woman and visited her home.

Living off Campus

Living off campus is another option, primarily for upperclass students, since they're better able to handle the independent nature of off-campus living. This could be the best of both worlds for some students: they get convenient access to everything offered on their campus yet also have the sanctuary of their off-campus residence. Off-campus living is preferred for married students or for first-year students who took off for a year or two before going to school and have grown accustomed to living separately from others. It's also great for siblings attending the same university.[5]

Finding a roommate can be a challenge for students living off campus. Suggest that your student ask the housing office or the commuter services department for guidance.[6] They may even have access to the same roommate-matching system their college uses to find a compatible roommate. (Note: they should also maintain contact with their commuter office if their university has one. They may be able to become a Commuter Assistant, serving the needs of commuting students—another leadership opportunity their school might offer!)

Your student will probably need help reading their lease, working out their expenses, and negotiating with their roommates on things such as who buys food and which food others can eat within the living space. This is even more important for off-campus students than those living on campus since they won't have an RA to help mediate any disputes. Have your student be clear about expectations and ask their roommates to be clear as well.

Another concern for off-campus students is getting off and on campus safely. Encourage your student to use well-lit walkways or to travel in groups if possible. Some campuses offer shuttles to common off-campus housing complexes, and your student should use those as well as ask for rides from friends.

While students living off campus rarely participate in campus activities the way on-campus students do, that's a mistake. On-campus activities of every kind such as clubs, organizations, and professional associations are for all students to enrich their lives and add to their learning.[7] Living a mile off campus shouldn't compromise that. Encourage your student to read the event flyers posted on campus, in email announcements, and on bulletin boards and make a point of attending some on-campus programs.

The same can be said of spending time with faculty. Faculty members don't know who lives where, and they are available to all students, regardless of residence. Your student should take advantage of that. I would say that off-campus students should spend as much time on campus in classrooms, laboratories, activities, and the library as on-campus students, the only difference being where they go at night. Just my advice.

Here's a final and very specific note. All students going away to school should have renters insurance. No college or landlord will be responsible for damage or theft of items other than the ones they supply. Laptops or other equipment damaged because of flooding or theft won't be covered on the landlord's or college's insurance policies. Insuring the contents of the apartment or residence hall room is your student's responsibility. Plus, it's very inexpensive. Don't let them be penny wise and pound foolish.

In Brief

Campus residence halls are there to support student learning and development, as well as provide a place to live.

Encourage your student to connect with their RA and to seek help from them when needed. That's their job.

Living off campus may require more work on your student's part, so be sure to help them with leases, setting up utilities, budgeting, and so forth.

If your student lives off campus, encourage them to be involved in campus activities, too.

Renter's insurance is a wise investment.

References

1. Cmcinfo. (n.d.). *Res Hall vs. Dorm*. Reslife. https://reslife.coloradomtn.edu/new-students/res-hall-vs-dorm/

2. Talley, F. J. (2019, July 10). *Roommates*. Helping Your College Student Succeed. http://www.collegeandparents.com/2019/07/10/roommates-in-college/

3. *Actually, We Do Deserve Accolades for Adulting*. (2020, March 5). Greatist. https://greatist.com/grow/adulting-meaning-validation

4. *College and University Residence Halls—Purpose of Residence Halls, Organization and Administration, Residence Hall Staffing, Residence Hall Student Government*. (n.d.). Education.stateuniversity.com. https://education.stateuniversity.com/pages/1845/College-University-Residence-Halls.html

5. University of the People. (n.d.). *Living on Campus vs Living off Campus: Weighing Your Options*. https://www.uopeople.edu/blog/living-on-campus-vs-living-off-campus/

6. Lemonade Insurance Agency. *Dorm Room, No More. Here Are 9 Tips for Living Off Campus*. https://www.lemonade.com/blog/living-off-campus/

7. Joseph, Tiffany & Trager, Sandy, (2019) *Pros and Cons of Living On Campus vs. Off Campus*, https://www.hercampus.com/school/broward/pros-and-cons-living-campus-vs-campus/

Chapter 9 - Life in a Diverse Community

One challenge of starting college is entering a brand-new community. Most students have been in one or multiple communities beforehand, but those were determined by their parents' work, military assignment, and so forth. And no one would deny that athletic teams or scout troops are communities in themselves. But they tend to be much smaller than college campuses. For many students, entering a community with thousands of students is daunting.

Chances are your student will be entering a college community with people who are very different from them. By different, I'm referring to differences of race, gender, sexual orientation, gender expression, and class. You can often find these demographics on the college's website, such as the number of students by race, gender, home address, and whether they are Hispanic or not. Campus demographics may also show the size of their students' high schools and whether those high schools are public or private. Take a look at these demographics, then think about your student's previous experience. Most likely, their campus may be quite different from their high school.

Difference also includes varying income levels, such as the contrast between students who are the first in their families who may earn a bachelor's degree versus those who have a long history of college attendance in the family. And there are also differences in political views and religious traditions among a college's students, staff, and faculty. Some people believe that saying "Let's get together in the sandbox and be friends and get along" is enough for new students. It isn't, because becoming a contributing and happy member of a college community doesn't happen all by itself.

Dealing with the "Isms"

Every member of a college community comes to the campus with experiences that tell them the people they should spend time with and the people they ought to avoid. This is the case even regarding people the student has never met before, which is why it's so hard to understand. Yes: students, staff, and faculty may turn away from people they've never met simply because they fit an image in their minds of someone they shouldn't spend time with based on stereotypes or strong biases. These are the "isms" at work. These include racism, sexism, ableism, classism, and others. As wonderful as our colleges and universities are, these "isms" still exist there. In fact, many of us spread them without realizing it. Your student will encounter these and may be a victim of one or more of them.

Here's an example: say your family is middle class to lower middle class. Your student receives financial aid, yet your family also foots their share of the bill. Your student is aware of the sacrifice you're making and is being careful with their money. Yet when they spend time with the new people they've met, they keep hearing about the cars and other toys they have and may be invited out several times to buy meals off campus. Your student knows they can't afford that, and they often decline. Eventually, those invitations may dry up. And they may even dry up if your student explains, "Hey, I don't have the money for that." Your student isn't being excluded because it's bad to budget their money. They may be excluded because by not having those resources, they may be someone the other students' parents warned them about. And if you think that's unfair to your student, you're correct.[1]

When a Caucasian student wonders why Black students don't just "act right" so they don't have to worry about being treated poorly in a predominately white town, that's an example of another "ism"—racism. Another one is a white person ignoring the fact that racial bias exists because they don't experience it themselves. Not seeing bias isn't the problem; it's denying that it happens to Black students that is the problem. That problem is played out in general society and on college campuses every single day. Black students know this, yet many who aren't Black deny it exists and think differently and negatively about Black students as a result.²

We talk sometimes about having privilege, meaning there are fewer barriers placed in front of someone because of their backgrounds. Males, for example, have a level of privilege and access that women don't have. But even if we are a male who is white and straight—major areas of privilege—being poor may hamper us. My advice for your student as they approach other people is to remember the areas in which those individuals *don't* have privilege. That will help your student work more successfully with people from a wide variety of backgrounds and prior experiences. Denying someone else's struggles because we have struggles of our own doesn't do anyone any good. For a straightforward explanation of this, I recommend Allen G. Johnson's book *Privilege, Power, and Difference*. The book is an easy read and one I used for six years while teaching a first-year seminar course.²

LGBTQ+

Your student may be attending a college at which students, staff, and faculty may identify as lesbian, gay, bisexual, transgender, queer, or something else. This is often indicated by the acronym LGBTQ+. If LGBTQ+ students, staff, and faculty are part of the college community your student attends, your student must treat them with respect. This may be tough when they see a person who clearly looks like a woman, yet identifies himself by male pronouns and goes by a name that they associated with being male. It may be even tougher when someone says they are "nonbinary," meaning they don't identify as either male or female. Your student doesn't have to agree with that individual, or even understand them, but they have to accept them if they choose to remain at that college. For more information about gender issues such as sexual orientation, gender identity, and gender expression, I'd suggest your student read *Privilege, Power, and Difference*. It explains diversity, equity, and inclusion in very clear language.

Of course, that's not the case for every college in the United States. In fact, many colleges in the United States or beyond are not welcoming to students who are LGBTQ+, and that's clear from their website, bathrooms, and campus rules. Their values—that they are less or not accepting of people who are LGBTQ+—are often reflected throughout the campus. This means when searching for colleges, you and your student should be aware of what values the college expresses regarding these issues. That's a huge part of "fit."

Social and Economic Class

In any college classroom, you will find students who are wealthy and those who are poor. To break that down, I recall a student at a college I worked at whose father was a very well-known executive in a multinational company. Her BMW convertible had a vanity license plate, and she was able to park it in the most exclusive parking area on campus because of her father's regular donations to the college. To be clear, the student was very nice and didn't flaunt her wealth unnecessarily, but it was hard not to be envious when I saw her BMW while driving my older Toyota.

This student was an RA, and another RA in the same complex had very few financial resources. Her family had been on public assistance, and she had both grants and loans to help her pay her tuition. She also came from a small rural community where every family struggled to get by. While she and the wealthier student managed to get along, they were from completely different worlds. The first student probably had no idea of how privileged she was, while the second couldn't ignore that. To her, she may as well have come from another planet.

The differences between these two students—as stark as they may seem—play out on college campuses every single day. Many students are in the middle: they have enough money to get by, yet their family had to make sacrifices so they could attend college. They probably don't know what it feels like to worry about getting their next meal, nor what it means to have their own American Express Black Card. Yet, they should find ways to connect with people on these economic extremes in a positive way while they're on campus. This will prepare them to handle that same diversity once they graduate. The fact is that any campus may feel very different for students depending on their social and economic class: that's a fact reported by Nathan Martin in his article about the privilege of ease.[3]

The *Journal of Personality and Social Psychology* reported on a study to understand the subtle ways colleges and universities actually discriminate against poorer students. For example, one of my previous colleges charged a fee for changing a course schedule after a particular date. This fee is designed to discourage students from making changes to their schedules on a whim. But what about the student who really needs to get out of a course because they're failing but can't because they can't afford the $25 fee? How about residence hall fines for something like having alcohol for an underage student? The affluent student can easily afford the fine, but the poor student can't. While no one actually says they want poor students to have less flexibility than affluent students, the richer student can afford several fines before it hurts.[4]

Your student's college campus also employs many people in service positions, including people who work in food service, in the campus store, on the grounds, and as custodians. Please encourage your student to treat these people with respect as well. Many people in these positions, particularly where they have lots of student contact, such as in the cafeteria, serve as informal mentors for students. I realized that myself while I was in college. The main custodian in the campus center was always addressed by his first name. Let's call him "Harold." Harold was a Black man, of about my father's age at the time, and I had no trouble doing what other students did and called him by his first name. That was until a good friend of mine was chatting with me and said to Harold: "How are you doing today, Mr. Martin?" I took notice of this and realized what I had been doing. Calling Harold Martin by his first name would have earned me a stern rebuke in my neighborhood, or a smack upside the head by my father. Maybe the other students at my college were privileged enough that a person in a service position would normally be called by his first name, but that wasn't how I was raised. The next time I saw him, I referred to him as Mr. Martin. He returned the greeting and smiled, showing his approval. That's a lesson I've remembered for more than forty years now.

Many of my students have told me how a staff person in the cafeteria helped them when they felt down, or referred them to get support, or celebrated when they had an academic success. People in service positions like this are acting as educators and supports to your students. Please be sure that your student treats them that way.

Political and Religious Diversity

I've grouped these together since often politics and religion are grouped together. On American college campuses, the majority of students who have a religious preference identify as Christian. This may or may not be an issue to students who identify as Jewish, Muslim, Hindu, or any number of other faith traditions. It also may not matter to those who are atheists, but it could. Remember privilege? Many don't think about privilege as being associated with religious traditions, but if you were to ask them to find a greeting card to celebrate Eid—the breaking of the fast during Ramadan—they'd have a hard time finding one. And because we've politicized religion so much, it's become difficult for young students to speak with people of other religious traditions without preconceived notions and biases coming up. But they should still make the effort, and many already are. *Religion News* reported on a new project that scores colleges on how much they welcome religious diversity, as seen by Jewish, Muslim, and Hindu students.[5] In fact, when colleges talk about diversity on campus, they often skip religious diversity.[6,7] But even at public universities, this is changing, as campuses seek to become more inclusive of the world's many religious traditions.

Political diversity is another hot-button issue for college campuses. The fact is that campuses are already diverse in terms of political beliefs. The question is how openly people can express their political views in a positive, engaging way that leads to dialogue rather than angry debate. To be honest, higher education is a work in progress in that way. Philanthropy Roundtable addresses that specifically in an intriguing article.[8] Andriana Taratsas, a student at Carleton College, bemoans this in her 2021 opinion piece in her college newspaper that sums up the challenge of political diversity. She says that some people just don't have the ability to listen to different views and rather attack others at the first sign of dissension.[9] I'm not surprised she feels this way.

There are even organizations, such as the Foundation for Individual Rights in Education (FIRE), that specifically support free expression on college campuses. What they most support, however—in my opinion—are the expression of more conservative views that they believe are systematically squashed on college campuses. They also oppose campus speech codes. These codes are often put in place to protect people from harassment, yet FIRE suggests that they usually inhibit speech by less popular views on campus, which inhibits dialogue. They also rate colleges in terms of their free speech.[10] Your student should understand that differences in political views are part of what college and university students, staff, and faculty talk about, and they should be prepared to be challenged for their views along the way.

What's a Student to Do?

In the tradition of challenging themselves so they can grow, I say your student should find a college community that feels comfortable and hits all, or most, of their check marks, such as major, distance from home, reputation, cost, and campus "feel." If they are concerned about their ability to fit in or find a specific need that pertains to their sexual identity, race, class, religion, or political beliefs, they should ask the college or university before making their final decision.

I'm not suggesting that students should only attend a college where nothing challenges their values or point of view—far from it. I believe we all grow as individuals when we are tested and encouraged to examine our values, understand where our views come from, and discover, perhaps, that we are unfairly biased against others. Your student can grow tremendously as a young adult when they spend time interacting meaningfully with people who are very different from them. However, only your student can determine how comfortable they will be in a given college community.

But they should understand something else: not every part of any college will be comfortable. There may be schools that seem like the perfect "fit" yet will still challenge them to work with types of people they've never seen before except on television. And whether your student is one of those who is more privileged or less privileged than others doesn't matter: once they enter a campus as a member of that college community, they have the responsibility and the opportunity to be a positive contributing member who treats people with respect and earns that respect from others. Maybe if more students embraced this responsibility and opportunity earlier, the differences that seem to divide us as a nation would shrink, rather than expand.

In Brief

Your student will likely encounter many people on campus who aren't like them. Encourage them to treat these students, staff, faculty, and guests with respect.

Not everyone comes to college with the same advantages . . . or challenges. Urge your student to recognize these differences and act in a way that raises everyone up.

Along the way, your student's view on difference may be challenged. While this may make them uncomfortable, when done properly and respectfully, this give-and-take of exploring values and perspectives is one of the many benefits of being part of a college community.

Take some time during college visits to ask about the college community and encourage your student to get out of their comfort zone and see how the campus feels. This will help them make the best college choice decision they can.

References

1. Johnson, A. G. (2006). *Privilege, Power, and Difference*. McGraw Hill.

2. Johnson, *Privilege, Power, and Difference*.

3. Martin, N. D. (2012). The Privilege of Ease: Social Class and Campus Life at Highly Selective, Private Universities. *Research in Higher Education*, 53(4), 426–452. https://www.jstor.org/stable/41475401

4. Chang, A. (2017, September 11). *The Subtle Ways Colleges Discriminate against Poor Students, Explained in a Cartoon.* Vox. https://www.vox.com/2017/9/11/16270316/college-mobility-culture

5. *A New Project Scores Colleges on How Much They Welcome Religious Diversity.* (2022, January 28). Religion News Service. https://religionnews.com/2022/01/28/a-new-project-scores-colleges-on-how-much-they-welcome-religious-diversity/

6. O'Donnell, G. (2020, March 17). *Religious Diversity is the Missing Piece in Campus DEI Work.* INSIGHT into Diversity. https://www.insightintodiversity.com/religious-diversity-is-the-missing-piece-in-campus-dei-work/;

7. Patel, E. (2007). Religious Diversity and Cooperation on Campus. *Journal of College and Character, 9*(2). https://doi.org/10.2202/1940-1639.1120

8. Merrill, J. P. (n.d.). *Fall 2016—Improving Political Diversity on Campus.* Philanthropy Roundtable. https://www.philanthropyroundtable.org/philanthropy-magazine/article/fall-2016-improving-political-diversity-on-campus

9. *Encouraging Political Diversity on Campus.* (2021, January 16). The Carletonian. https://thecarletonian.com/2021/01/16/encouraging-political-diversity-on-campus/

10. *2021 College Free Speech Rankings.* (n.d.). FIRE. https://www.thefire.org/research/publications/student-surveys/2021-college-free-speech-rankings/

Chapter 10 - Safety and Other Things You Worry About

Parents and family members worry about their students, whether they're at home or at college. But when they're in college, we often worry even more about their not being accepted into a group, experimenting with alcohol and other drugs, and becoming sexually active. These concerns are understandable and real, and you're not the first parent or family member to worry about them.[1]

But here's the rub: college campuses often *feel* very safe. The students are friendly, some buildings have controlled access, and the generally open nature of college campuses gives students and others a false sense of security. Many staff and faculty fall victim to the sense that "those things don't happen here," including me. But that doesn't mean we're right. I rewrote this chapter at the urging of one of my beta readers to include more information on campus safety in addition to sections on alcohol, drugs, and mental health, so here we are.

College students often feel they are invulnerable, and since "nothing bad ever happens here," they make mistakes in how they live their lives. Many don't lock their doors unless prompted, they often walk alone at night, and they don't secure their belongings when they leave them somewhere. They also may not question when a nice person hands them something to drink. These are things they probably wouldn't do anywhere else, such as a coffee shop, but they do them at college.

Think About Safety *Before* They Choose a College

As I mentioned before, students can't count on college campuses being any safer than their home communities. This is what led to the

Cleary Act, designed to ensure that students, staff, and faculty are aware of the crimes committed on campus and to lay out the support and legal resources available to victims of campus crime.[2] Every college in the United States reports their crime statistics annually and features those statistics on their websites. They should be easy to find.

You and your student can use this information during the college search process. You both may feel better choosing a campus located in a safer community or with lower crime statistics. The last thing you want is for your student to be so concerned about safety that they can't take advantage of all that their college has to offer or to be so stressed that they can't study.

This is another reason that taking a tour of campus and getting a feel for the college and surroundings is important. There's no better way for your student to test their comfort level than to visit the place they'll spend the next few years. In fact, try to spend time on the campus at night, too. This may increase their sense of security if there are plenty of lights, activities, and safety resources on campus, such as blue lights. Or it may raise additional questions about campus safety.[3] Both results will help them make the right decision about which college to choose.

Public Safety

The office that handles campus safety and security might be known as the department of public safety, police, or safety and security. This is the first line of defense and safety for students, staff, and faculty on campus. Some departments have police powers while others have training that gives them specific powers above that of an average citizen.[4] Your student's public safety department may also have a mixture of people in it: some with arrest powers and some without. Colleges determine the kind of department they want. All colleges, however, should have a connection to local and state law enforcement agencies for matters that exceed their authority. Only you and your student can determine if the department meets your needs and expectations.

Safewise suggests that one step all students should take is to visit their college's department of public safety (I'll use that as an umbrella term for campus safety and law enforcement).[5] Safewise has other suggestions as well, some of which are simple common sense. For example, they suggest that students lock their belongings, whether in their car or residence hall room. Further, they urge students to take special precautions at night or when getting out of their cars.

Safewise also suggests that students should stock up on safety supplies, such as personal alarms and whistles. Another of their suggestions, however, is worth greater attention. Safewise says that students who choose to carry mace or pepper spray should test it periodically to make sure it works. However, your student should first find out if pepper spray is permitted on their campus. Many colleges have rules against students having weapons on campus, and pepper spray is considered a weapon. That means your student may receive a penalty for using it against campus rules. That's something to think about.

The International Association for Campus Law Enforcement offers guidelines to strengthen campus law enforcement and to partner with your student in maintaining their safety.[6] One newer campus resource many schools use is a campus alert system. Brand names of these systems include CampusSafe, Campus Shield, Guardly, and others.[7] These services provide alerts when incidents occur on campus or when a campus needs to go on lockdown. If your student's campus offers one of these services, please encourage them to use it.

Alcohol and Other Drugs

First, give up the notion that all college students drink: that isn't true. What *is* true is that college students often have the "perfect storm," which leads them to experiment with alcohol and other drugs. They're away from their parents and in a less supervised environment than their family home. They're also around new people and looking for ways to fit in. They're seeking acceptance, and one way is to take part in all the things they *think* college students are supposed to do. I've worked hard over the years telling students that they don't have to drink to fit in, and in fact, they may gain more respect if they make rational choices about what they'll do and what they won't. Our daughter, who served as an RA for three years, was livid when, during orientation, she kept hearing full-time staff say: "We know you're going to drink."[8,9] I heard those same messages during parent orientation and was equally annoyed. My unvoiced response was: "No. They *don't*."

Students also don't have to use more dangerous drugs, such as marijuana, cocaine, or methamphetamine. The vast majority of students don't indulge in these, despite what you may see on TV or on social media, though many students will know someone who could get them one or more of these drugs. Every college has prevention and recovery programs or access to larger programs in their community should your student need them. And despite the Family Educational Rights and Privacy Act restrictions, your student's college will contact you when things become life threatening or compromise the ability of your student to remain in school.

Before your student gets to that critical point—the point where they're on campus and don't know what to do or how to say no—take the time to talk with them about your expectations and about all the temptations they will encounter in college.[10,11] If they're already aware of these and also aware of your stance on alcohol or drugs, talk about them anyway. Impress upon them the fact that these distractions will make it harder for them to reach the goals they've set for themselves. Also, let them know that if they stumble—such as get drunk or find themselves with a judicial charge—that they should talk to you. Sure, you may be disappointed and angry with them. But temper your anger or disappointment with the fact that at their age, they will make mistakes that will help them learn. And one thing you don't want them to do is to close off communication with you when they need you the most.

An Ounce of Prevention

Many colleges have an amnesty policy. These encourage students to get the help they need in case of potential emergency—especially those that may result from alcohol or drug abuse. Here's how it works. Let's say a student has consumed too much alcohol and is unconscious and in danger of alcohol poisoning. Since underage drinking is against campus rules, other students may be afraid to ask for help for their friend who is drunk for fear that their friend—or they—will get in trouble. Campus amnesty policies state that students who report alcohol or other drug abuse to protect themselves or others won't be penalized by the campus conduct system.[12] These policies encourage students to get the help they need.

Let's Talk About Sex

Sex is another taboo subject for students and parents, for obvious reasons. I don't know any parent who doesn't worry about the time when their student becomes sexually active.[8] Students often regard physical intimacy as a necessary part of affection when they're adolescents, yet they may be unable to handle the emotional attachments that come with it. They may also feel pressure to become sexually active for the same reasons students feel pressured to try alcohol or other drugs. And we worry about harassment and sexual assault, too.

All U.S. colleges follow what's known as Title IX guidelines, which prohibit sexual misconduct, including but not limited to sexual harassment, sexual assault, and rape.[13] Title IX offices also develop programs that teach students safer sex practices and decision making so that students who choose not to be sexually active are supported. As family members, we need open lines of communication so that our students can ask us questions about sex as emerging adults, not solely as our children. This is one of the most difficult challenges of parenting a college student. But it is better to understand that these pressures exist and be involved with them on this journey than to ignore the challenges because "my student wouldn't do that." Perhaps they won't, but that's not a chance I suggest you take.

A Final Note on Safety

Yes, going to college will present your students with new temptations and challenges that will worry you as their parent. Please keep the lines of communication open, allow for a few stumbles, and encourage your student to use the campus resources designed to keep them safe. Also, if you have concerns about your student's physical or mental health, don't hesitate to contact their college and speak with a member of the staff about your concerns.

In Brief

Encourage your student to think about safety on campus from day one. While colleges are often safer than surrounding communities, they are still part of that community. Make sure they're aware of that.

Your student should lock their doors, be cautious when walking alone, and walk with friends at night for extra safety: things you've probably told them for years.

If their university offers a service that provides campus alerts, encourage them to subscribe to it.

Your student doesn't have to drink or use drugs to fit in. Support them as they try to make mature decisions and stay true to themselves. And urge them to get help for themselves and their friends if they've had too much to drink.

Being sexually active isn't just about sex. Have frank conversations with your student about intimacy before they go to college and while they're enrolled.

References

1. Talley, F. J. (2018, July 6). *Cheers, Not Tears.* Helping Your College Student Succeed. http://www.collegeandparents.com/2018/07/06/cheers-not-tears/

2. *Details of the Clery Act.* (n.d.). University of California: Office of the President. https://www.ucop.edu/ethics-compliance-audit-services/compliance/clery-act/clery-act-details.html

3. Wood, S. (2022, November 11). College Campus Safety: Questions to Ask. US News and World Report. https://www.usnews.com/education/best-colleges/applying/articles/college-campus-safety-questions-to-ask

4. Review of *Enhancing Campus Safety and Security*. (2014, March 14). Bureau of Justice Assistance. https://bja.ojp.gov/program/enhancing-campus-safety-and-security/overview

5. Edwards, R. (2021, October 20). Review of *9 Ways to Stay Safe on Your College Campus*. Safewise. https://www.safewise.com/blog/9-easy-ways-to-stay-safe-on-your-college-campus/

6. International Association for Campus Law Enforcement. (n.d.). https://www.iaclea.org

7. Button, K. (2014, March 14). Review of *10 Mobile Apps Making Campuses Safer*. HigheredDive.com. https://www.highereddive.com/news/10-mobile-apps-making-campuses-safer/241575/

8. Talley, F. J. (2018, July 6). *First Time for Everything*. Helping Your College Student Succeed. http://www.collegeandparents.com/2018/07/06/first-time-for-everything/;

9. Talley, F. J. (2018, July 11). *No, They Don't Have to Drink*. Helping Your College Student Succeed. http://www.collegeandparents.com/2018/07/11/no-they-dont-have-to-drink/

10. *How to Talk to Your Student About Alcohol*. (n.d.). EVERFI. https://everfi.com/substance-abuse-prevention-resources-for-parents/how-to-talk-to-your-student-about-alcohol/

11. Talley, F. J. (2018, July 27). *Work on Communication Before School Starts*. Helping Your College Student Succeed. http://www.collegeandparents.com/2018/07/27/effective-communication-with-your-college-student/

12. *Alcohol Amnesty*. (2019). Penn State Student Affairs. https://studentaffairs.psu.edu/health-wellness/alcohol-amnesty

13. U.S. Department of Education. (2018). *Title IX and Sex Discrimination*. Ed.gov.

https://doi.org/http://www.ed.gov/about/offices/list/ocr/docs/tix_dis.html

Chapter 11 - Academic Success in College

Parents of college students want their student to succeed. We've all heard horror stories (or perhaps we *were* the horror story) where students go to college and tank in the first semester. There are many reasons students don't succeed in college, and not just because of poor preparation. Transitioning to the demands of college often points out gaps that may exist between even the strongest student's prior achievements and what's required of them in college.

Here's a case in point. I mentioned in an earlier chapter that many students are shocked with the amount of time they have to spend studying and reading outside of class.[1] That was my problem years ago. I was going to class consistently and reading the materials beforehand, but I had never highlighted anything in a book and didn't know how to use highlighting as a learning tool. I was reading the material to get through it, *not* reading to understand it. Students in high school can get by with reading to get through it: that doesn't fly in college. Students need to learn very specific academic behaviors in college in order to succeed, which I'll explain in this chapter.

Another reason students don't succeed in college is that they don't feel connected to the school. "Connected" in this case is defined as feeling as though they fit in, that they have a home, and that they're valued. When students don't feel validated as individuals, they begin to lose focus and motivation and don't follow through on using those academic skills they already have.[2,3] The same applies to their social selves: if they don't feel they are part of something bigger than themselves, they may isolate themselves and not reach out to others because in their minds, what's the point? That's why RAs hold so many get-acquainted activities in their residence halls—so students can create meaningful connections with other students.[4]

Students are also more likely to feel that it's worth it to go to college and stay enrolled if they have a goal in mind. A goal might be a career they want or a purpose, such as helping youth or reducing poverty. It may also be their commitment to solving a complex medical or scientific problem.[5] When students have goals and see even a tiny relationship between their coursework, majors, and those goals, they will remain enrolled, all other things remaining the same. But a student who can't see a connection between themselves and their goals may leave a school that in all other ways is perfect for them.

But what if a student doesn't have clearly defined goals or any clue about their major? How do we help that student develop goals and a sense of purpose? This is the reason colleges have career centers and academic advising offices. If there's anything I can teach you about career planning or academic advising it's this: when your student says they want to major in neuroscience, I suggest you don't ask about what they'll do with a major in neuroscience. Instead, ask what they see themselves doing in five or ten years and then follow that up by asking how people in that career get there.[6] You'd then be within your rights to ask if neuroscience is the best or only way to get there. Most times, you will find a clear connection between career and major, but if you don't, ask how your student came up with neuroscience as a major instead of something else. Career development and academic advising professionals will also ask the same questions. Also, don't be too concerned if your student takes a bit more time figuring out their major or future career: most students in college change their major two or three times and can still graduate on time.

What Successful Students Do

Rather than focus on why students fail, let's focus on what successful students do. The first thing successful students do is become active learners. They direct their education and don't wait for others to direct it for them. Here's an example regarding academic advising. Colleges and universities assign academic advisors to their students, and the students are responsible for setting up meetings with their advisors before they register for courses for the upcoming term.[7,8] One of the most perplexing things students can do is to walk into that advising meeting and ask: "What should I take next semester?" They're within their rights to do so, but they should have some idea of what is ahead in their academic timeline.[7] Successful students listen when their major is explained to them, so they understand the required courses they need to take and when. Each time they complete a course, they should mark it off their list (most colleges provide these) so they come into an advising meeting asking not what to take but instead if their proposed schedule they developed makes sense.

Successful students also need to understand prerequisites for certain college courses. At my last college, the psychology major was easy to understand (for me) until 2021. Two required courses were Writing and Research Methods 1 and 2. Students had to complete these courses before they could take the two laboratory courses required during their junior or senior years. I urged my psychology majors to take the Writing and Research 1 and 2 during their sophomore year so they could take at least one lab course during the junior year. If they didn't do that, they'd be taking both lab courses during their senior year along with their two-semester independent research project required for graduation. When a psychology major met with me to plan their first semester sophomore year without the first part of the Writing and Research course, I asked them why. Advisors clarify and offer advice so students can build their own schedule from scratch—even if the schedules they build aren't very good at first. What matters is for the student to take the initiative: that's what leads to their eventual success.[9]

Self-direction truly is key for successful college students. They have to move from a more passive style of learning in high school that is very teacher focused to one that is more teacher led or directed with lots of opportunities for student involvement.[10] First-year students are notorious for saying little in class and not engaging in class discussion. Why should they? They didn't have to in high school. Only the "smart kids" did that. Well, guess what? Now they're in college and *are* one of the smart kids. Best get to talking. My students became comfortable with me asking a discussion question in class and saying "I've got time" if no one responded. I wanted to make it clear that I wasn't going to give them more answers. Instead, I was going to wait until someone addressed the questions so that discussion could continue. This classroom discussion and "exercising" with class materials is what often distinguishes college classrooms from high school classrooms. This is often uncomfortable for new students, and if your student is shy, encourage them to answer or ask at least some questions in class. They could also choose to be the second or third person to offer a comment in class. That way, they aren't stepping too far out of their comfort zone, but they're still engaging with the material. Faculty notice when a student says virtually nothing in class. That neither helps the student in terms of grade nor in terms of becoming more engaged in college, and engagement is key.

Something else successful students do is they tend to sit toward the front of the classroom.[11] Discourage your student from sitting toward the back of the classroom. Studies show that the farther back a student sits, the lower their grade. Sitting in the "front of the middle" is close to the front, without being in the professor's face, and should be comfortable for most students, even the shy ones.

Time Management

Every incoming student talks about time management, and they've heard this term thrown around constantly.[1] Many also worry about managing their time because they haven't had to do it much before. I give my students a blank schedule form that includes all twenty-four hours for a day, seven days a week, or one hundred sixty-eight hours. I've included a copy of the form in the appendix. The blank schedule encourages them to write down everything they do over the course of the week. This includes their classes, meals, sleep, laundry, and all study times in addition to exercise times, time with friends, and so forth. Most students don't fill these out completely. For example, I ask them to identify what they're studying each hour. The results are often telling. Most of them only identify about two hours per night for studying, which isn't enough for a college student. Successful students spend about four to six hours a day in academic pursuits, or about two to two and a half hours for every hour they spend in class.

This means around thirty to thirty-seven and a half hours per week studying for a student carrying a fifteen-credit load. Spread over seven days, this is between five and six hours a day. While this shocks new students, I tell them they're in class for about three to four hours a day and can easily spend an hour in the morning, an hour and a half in the afternoon, and then two and a half hours in the evening studying. This is without infringing on time to work out, hang out with friends, eat meals, and so forth. As one successful student of mine said to first-year students: "You have enough time in the week for everything you need and want to do." But this requires discipline and a plan.

Planners

I recommend that students use planners. And it doesn't matter which brand they choose, so don't splurge on some three-hundred-dollar system that "every student uses." Your student should use a system that works for them and any system that reminds them what to do and when can work. If you have an office job where you've got meetings and other assignments with deadlines, you're familiar with this. Students in college need a system as well, and it's especially important for new students.

Being Selfish with Their Time

Successful students are also selfish with their time. By selfish, I mean developing a system that works for them and sticking to it, regardless of peer pressure. For example, when they're in the middle of a productive study session, students need to say "Not right now, thanks" when a roommate asks them to go out. That doesn't mean your student can't be spontaneous: it means they have to decide each time if the change in their study schedule can be accommodated or if it's going to throw them off. If it's the latter, they should learn to say, "Not now, thanks. I'm finally making progress on this homework and I don't want to stop. Next time." Not only will they be more successful, but they may teach their roommate a thing or two about studying as well.

College Notetaking

Most new students don't come to college with great notetaking skills. The next chapter in this book focuses on notes and notetaking systems. Keep in mind that what they hear in class, both during the professor's lecture or from class discussion, is all fair game on an exam. Writing what is happening in class—the main points of the reading, the discussion, and differences between the two—are essential in helping students learn what they've being taught. I also strongly encourage students to write down some of the more understandable points made by their peers since that may help them as well.

Many students either write down too much or too little in their notes. Students who write down too much find they have far too much to go through before an exam. So when they're studying, it's like they're reading the book all over again. Students who write down too little often miss important points from the lecture and discussion and are equally handicapped before the exam. And this is an important point: taking notes is important *because it prepares students to pass the exam* or complete the other assignments required in the course. They aren't taking notes to make themselves happy or to show other students how pretty they can make their paper. They are taking notes to help them study later. Remind them of that.

The many systems of notetaking are expanded in the next chapter, with references to explain them further. Share these with your student to help them find a system that works for them. Remember, successful students always use a system.

Balance

I'll speak more about balance and wellness in a later chapter, but remind your student that while you want them to succeed academically, they won't succeed if they're unhappy, if they aren't eating well, or if they aren't getting the amount of sleep and recreation they need. For example, if your student studies into the late hours too much and catches a cold, they won't be able to study effectively. Your student should be spending time in the gym or exercising every day or two as well, and they can make great friends while doing so. Remind them not to spend too much time on these activities. They should not be playing basketball three hours a day, five days a week unless they've in an official practice. Most students should be spending those three hours studying biology or economics rather than dribbling.

And even before-college couch potatoes should become more physical while in college. They won't have the required physical education courses they had during high school and may gain more weight than they'd like. No shade to my colleagues, but college professors and administrators aren't known for their impressive physiques—me included. Yet, many of us have an activity regimen that keeps us healthy and able to perform our jobs. College students need that as much as we do.

Two Basic Rules

Please pass these two rules on to your student. They are two rules I've employed in my scholars' program for underrepresented students. The first is to go to class: they can't take part if they aren't there.[9,10] Unless they're in a huge lecture hall, faculty notice when students aren't there, and especially when it's the same students who are missing day after day. Even without a seating chart, we remember which seat tends to be empty, since students usually sit in the same seats every day. Also, if a student comes to my office for assistance after missing several classes, I'm happy to help them, but I'll notice if the things they're struggling with are things I covered when they were absent. I'll also make a point of asking them about their attendance so they see the connection between attendance and understanding. I don't browbeat the student about this, but I do help them understand that *attendance matters*. Some colleges even require attendance, especially for first-year students. If not, faculty may require it on their own. I give my students three absences before they count against them, and most students respect that. To be honest, I still don't like it when they aren't there, and most faculty agree with me. Encourage your student to go to every class, and if they can't make it because they're sick, make sure the faculty member knows that, *before* class, not afterward. Most faculty will be understanding, even as they hold to their attendance policy. But at least they won't be angry about the absence.

A second rule is a tougher one for students who are perfectionists, and that is, "turn stuff in."[9-10] (My associate director coined this but didn't use the word "stuff.") It's tough for new students to follow the second rule because we've told them as parents not to turn in something that isn't the best. That's to motivate them to do their best at all times. On the other hand, not turning something in because it isn't perfect and taking a zero on the assignment makes no sense. Even something that only earns the student 20 percent (and that's rare—most faculty will give far more to substandard work) is better than a zero. Where this gets difficult is when students obsess over making their work perfect because "this is college." One of my students said it best: "Strive for progress, not perfection." It's not about perfection, so pass that on to your student. And if they ask you to read a paper just to get your reaction or feedback, be honest, constructive, and respectful in your response. This will encourage them to ask for help in college, another sign of a successful student.

In Brief

College is tougher than high school, which your student already knows. Talk with them about giving the right amount of time to their academics.

Feeling connected to the campus matters, too. Encourage them to attend programs and develop social connections.

Successful students are active learners: they ask questions in class and contribute to the class discussions. This is expected of everyone, not just the top students.

Encourage them to consult often with their academic advisor to develop a multiyear course plan.

Time management is one of the toughest skills for new students to learn. Urge them to purchase a planner or develop a system to plan their days, that they will follow.

Teach them two basic rules: go to class and turn stuff in.

References

1. Talley, F. J. (2019, February 18). *Taking Control of Their Time as College Students.* Helping Your College Student Succeed. http://www.collegeandparents.com/2019/02/18/taking-control-of-their-time-as-new-college-students/

2. Inkelas, K., Daver, Z., Vogt, K., & Leonard, J. (2007). Review of *Living-Learning Programs and First-Generation College Students' Academic and Social Transition to College. Research in Higher Education, 48*(4);.

3. Pascarella, E. T., & Terenzini, P. T. (2005). *How College Affects Students. Volume 2: A Third Decade of Research.* Jossey-Bass.

4. *How to Truly Succeed in College.* (2019). ThoughtCo. https://www.thoughtco.com/how-to-succeed-in-college-793219

5. *I'm Struggling in College . . . Now What? 6 Tips for Getting Back on Track.* (n.d.). Rasmussen College. https://www.rasmussen.edu/student-experience/college-life/struggling-in-college/

6. Talley, F. J. (2018, July 13). *Why Is She Taking So Many Courses That Aren't in Her Major?* Helping Your College Student Succeed. http://www.collegeandparents.com/2018/07/13/why-is-she-taking-so-many-courses-that-arent-in-her-major/

7. Talley, F. J. (2018, October 21). *What Academic Advising Is Supposed to Mean.* Helping Your College Student Succeed. http://www.collegeandparents.com/2018/10/21/whats-academic-advising/;

8. Kelci Lynn Lucier, Kelci Lynn. (2011). *What College Students Who Need Help Academically Should Do.* US News & World Report. https://www.usnews.com/education/blogs/the-college-experience/2011/10/26/what-college-students-who-need-help-academically-should-do

9. Talley, F. J. (2020, February 4). *The Best Academic Advising Appointment.* Helping Your College Student Succeed. http://www.collegeandparents.com/2020/02/04/the-best-academic-advising-appointment/

10. *Ten Tips on How to Be a Successful College Student.* (2017, January 20). Stukent. https://www.stukent.com/successful-college-student/

11. *Tips for College Success.* (n.d.). EducationQuest. https://www.educationquest.org/college-students/tips-for-college-success/

Chapter 12 - Taking Notes in College

It's a fact of college life that students attend classes and take notes. And, of course, successful college students also take notes on their reading.

According to Utah State University's Academic Resource Center, whether taken on paper or on a computer, good notes:

- Are organized.
- Distinguish main points from details.
- Include examples.
- Indicate lecture patterns.
- Allow for self-testing.
- Stand the test of time.
- Use abbreviations.[1]

More than anything, notes taken in class should help students study and succeed in class. That's what they're for. And the primary reason to take good notes is that there is simply too much information presented and discussed in college classrooms to succeed without them. Students who believe they're "getting it" in class and don't need to take notes at the same time are fooling themselves. When your student says "I don't need to take notes in class" or "it's really just common sense" (I hear this a lot for psychology and sociology classes), do a full stop: students who say this and don't take notes because it would be "a waste of time" are unlikely to succeed in college. There are many great notetaking methods. I'll review five of the most popular ones here.

The Outline Method

The first method is the Outline Method, or as I was taught, Statement/ P.I.E, with PIE standing for Proofs, Information and Examples. Laia Hanau developed the method in 1960.[2] I've also seen "PIE" referred to as "proof, information, and explanation." Using this method, students arrange their notes so that major points or statements take up the entire line, while points under the major statements are indented, in much the way we learned how to outline. This method works because students can see the most important points at a glance. Outline notes might look like Figure 1.

Outline Method Using Chickering's Vectors

```
Chickering's Vectors of Development
1. Developing Competence
Three types
    Intellectual
        Ability to understand, analyze and synthesize
    Manual
        Physical ability to accomplish tasks
    Interpersonal
        Working with and establishing relationships with others
2. Managing Emotions
    Handling intense emotions, e.g., fear, anger, happiness, sadness
    Recognize balance between self-awareness and self-control
3. Movement Through Autonomy Toward Interdependence
Two types
    Emotional
        Ability to risk relationships as they pursue their interests or convictions
    Instrumental
        Solving problems on their own and establishing their physical independence
        "Adulting"
```

Figure 1. The Outline Method

Figure 1 about body language shows how posture, body language, and nonverbal cues can make an oral presentation more effective or less effective, and because the notes are well-organized, they are easy to understand. With the outline method, students write statements in short, bullet fashion, rather than full sentences. This is also much faster than trying to write everything a professor says in class. The outline method is also the basis for other methods of notetaking, such as the Cornell Method.

The Cornell Method

The Cornell Method was developed in the 1940s by Walter Pauk, then at Cornell University.[3] This method requires students to divide their note pages into three sections, as seen in Figure 2.

Name, Date Topic, Class	
Cues and Keywords	NOTES taken during class (using outline method)
These may be written during or after class	
	• Main points
	• Bullet points
Anticipated exam questions	• Diagrams/ charts
	• Abbreviate
Main ideas or people	• Paraphrase
	• Outlines
Key terms	• Leave space between topics
	• Write only on one side of the paper
Quotes	
	You may cover the notes, then use the cues and
Used for review and study	keywords to see how much you remember, or cover the
	keywords and generate the notes from memory.
	Summary
Written after class. This is a brief summary highlighting the main points in the notes on this page.	

Figure 2. The Cornell Method

Students take notes in outline form in the large section using bullet points, putting minor points under major points. After class, students review their notes and place key words and definitions in the left-hand column, with a summary of the major points in a sentence or two on the bottom. Figure 3 demonstrates a real-life example of Cornell notes in action. They were produced using a handwriting-like font for ease of reading. Your student would be writing them in longhand.

Amy Cohen	5/17/2008
The Near East	Page 4

Jericho	JERICHO
	1st city developed
	Before Jericho, people were mobile
3 req'ments for	
dev'ment of cities	Three requirements for dev'ment of cities
Water	1. Water = 1st req'ment
	- cities built by lakes, rivers
Agriculture	2. Agriculture = 2nd req'ment
	- division of labor: women planted, men hunted
Protection	3. Protection = 3rd req'ment
	- walls of Jericho built to protect farms and water from invaders
	- walls built 7800 BC
	- city survived 800 years

SUMMARY: Jericho is significant as first city. Requirements for development of cities are water, agriculture and protection.

Figure 3. The Cornell Method at Work

This is a great example of Cornell at work. The points are simple and organized, and you can imagine a student covering the large part of the paper and trying to generate what's in the middle to see how much they remember. This is the method I began using during my doctoral studies, though I didn't know it had a name. Your student can visit several websites to generate Cornell Method sheets that are already separated into three sections, such as through Incompetech.[4]

The Mind Map Method

A third popular method is mind mapping, which is a visual representation of notes and class discussion. Students represent ideas on the printed page showing the connections between related concepts. Remember the outline method example on body language and oral presentations? Here are mind mapping notes on the topic of Chickering's Vectors of Development (Figure 4).

Figure 4. The Mind Map Method

This method works best when a lecture is well-organized. A student going into a class where the topics aren't as well defined may have a tough time using mind mapping, but this method may be a godsend to visual learners. And there's nothing to say students can't transcribe or copy their notes using this method, particularly if it helps them remember key points before an exam.

The Chart Method

The fourth method is called charting, which is what it sounds like. Figure 5 provides an example of a basic chart.

Presidents of the United States 1960-1980

President	Years in Office	Vice President	Interesting Facts
John F. Kennedy	1961-1963	Lyndon Johnson	Assassinated in office in 1963; youngest president to be elected to office at 42
Lyndon B. Johnson	1963-1969	Hubert Humphrey (only since 1965)	Accelerated war in Vietnam; started "Great Society Programs"
Richard Nixon	1969-1974	Spiro Agnew (1969-1973) Gerald Ford, 1973-1974)	Only US president to resign the office; first to use 25th amendment to fill a vacant vice presidency
Gerald Ford	1974-1977	Nelson Rockefeller	Pardoned former president Nixon, and offered conditional pardon for men who had evaded the military draft by leaving the country
James "Jimmy" Carter	1977-1981	Walter Mondale	Only US president to graduate from US Naval Academy; brokered Camp David Accords between Palestinians and Israelis

Figure 5. The Chart Method

Students create charts that help them organize important aspects of a concept, person, or era. Here's another example, using nations of the world.

Nations of the World By Total Area (Land and Water)

Nation & Capitol	Total Area (mi²)	Population	Flag
Russia, Moscow	6,601,670	144,713,314	
Canada, Ottawa	3,855,100	38,454,327	
United States, Washington DC	3,796,742	338,289,857	
China, Beijing	3,705,407	1,425,887,337	
Brazil, Brasilia	3,287,956	215,313,498	

Figure 6. The Chart Method for Nations of the World

This method works well for subjects like history, economics, or any subject with a great deal of vocabulary. It also allows for easy comparisons or summaries of information. Charts are easy to create and require little writing.

The Super Notes Method

Super notes is a method often used in the sciences. It is a combination of notes from class, a student's reading, and any other experience with the material, such as from a study group. Students create super notes after doing their before-class reading, attending class, and taking notes. They put everything together into a stronger, more comprehensive document. Super notes should be complete enough for the student to teach the lesson they just learned. Here is an example of Super Notes from a student at St. Mary's College of Maryland (Figure 7).[5]

location of receptor protein
1. cell surface / transmembrane receptors: hydrophilic ligand
2. intracellular receptor: hydrophobic ligand
- class of receptor protein (all cell surface)??
  2. g-protein coupled receptor:
     ○ receptor protein has 7 transmembrane domains
     ○ often involve in response to drugs
     ○ ex. olfactory, immune, neurotransmitters
     ○ uses g-protein as an intermediate to act indirectly on other proteins such as gated ion channels or enzymes
       ■ ligand binds to receptor protein
       ■ conformational change in receptor shape occurs
       ■ g-protein phosphorylates GDP to make GTP → becomes active
       ■ domains of g-protein dissociate and act on effector protein
       ■ effector protein often releases second messenger such as cAMP or Ca2+ which can change shape or behavior of proteins
     ○ G protein subunits (activators) activate effector proteins to produce second messengers
     ○ Concept mapping the terms:

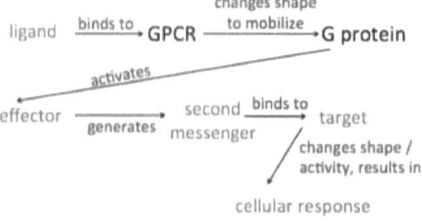

5

Figure 7. The Super Notes Method

This looks like a textbook, which is in some ways the point. Super Note are usually typed, and include charts, diagrams and other tools created from several sources to aid in studying and memory retention. Creating Super Notes, while time intensive, focuses students' minds and requires them to develop a deep understanding of the material and the relationships between concepts. And those who use them find them indispensable.

Methods for notetaking aren't stand-alone, either. As mentioned earlier, the Cornell method is the outline method with added structure. And students can also use the outline method and then create a chart to help them remember important points and comparisons before an exam. The key is for students to find the method or methods that work for them and use them consistently. Finding and using these notetaking methods flexes every student's "mental muscles" and primes them for success.

To help your student, ask them what method or methods they're using, and if they're not sure what to use or how to use it, refer them to the proper campus resources to help them, including their professors.

In Brief

The notes your student takes in class should be easy to understand and should help prepare them for taking their tests.

Encourage your student to develop a system. The ones outlined in the chapter should help.

If your student knows a classmate who takes great notes, they should ask to see them and learn the system that the student uses.

Your student's campus has several people or offices designed to help with their notes, including their course professors and their advisor. Encourage them to use these resources.

References

1. Review of *College Notetaking: Another Academic Success Key!* (n.d.). Utah State University Academic Resource Center.

2. *Learning Can Be As Easy As "Statement-Pie" She Says.* (n.d.). Ann Arbor District Library. https://aadl.org/node/74446

3. *Cornell Note Taking—The Best Way To Take Notes Explained.* (2022, September 19). GoodNotes. https://medium.goodnotes.com/study-with-ease-the-best-way-to-take-notes-2749a3e8297b

4. *Free Online Graph Paper / Cornell Note-taking Lined.* (n.d.). Incompetech. https://incompetech.com/graphpaper/cornelllined/

5. Shirvan, L. (2018). *Super Notes on Receptor Proteins.* Used with permission.

Chapter 13 - A Typical Day

While there is no typical day for an American college student or a student anywhere else in the world, I want to open the window and suggest what your student's day-to-day life might look like. Parents of college students, particularly those who weren't able to attend college themselves, rarely know how their students spend their time.[1,2] I hope this example is helpful.

First, recognize that while your student will only be in class for fifteen to twenty hours per week, that's not all they'll do academically. Students should spend about two to two-and-a-half hours outside of class for every hour in class, and I'll show that in my example.[3] To make this easy, I've named your student "Jamie."

Your Student, Hour by Hour (Perhaps)

8:30 a.m. Jamie wakes up a mere thirty minutes before their first class, which is English. For a student who got up before 6:00 a.m. for years, this may shock you. Jamie gets up, shakes out the cobwebs, brushes their teeth (may shower or not!), and then slithers into class at two minutes before 9:00.

9:00–9:50 a.m. Attends English class.

10:00–10:30 a.m. Heads to the library to search for an article they will need for a paper in their History class. This takes them about thirty minutes. When that's over, they head to the coffee shop to buy a latte.

10:50–11:00 a.m. Time to drop by the office of their biology professor, hoping to pick up a copy of their graded lab report.

11:00–11:50 a.m. Psychology class. This is Jamie's intended major, so they always pay greater attention in this class than in any other. During class, they raise their hand and participate in discussion three times and leave with a smile on their face.

12:00–1:00 p.m. Back to the library to read over their history notes and the reading from the night before. History is Jamie's most challenging class because they have to memorize so many dates. They go over what they highlighted the day before and review the study questions at the end of the chapter, recognizing that for two of the questions, they couldn't find the answer.

1:00–1:30 p.m. Lunch. This is Jamie's first meal of the day and they savor it, sitting with a friend.

1:30–2:00 p.m. Continues work on History readings before class.

2:00–2:50 p.m. History class (Western Civilization). Jamie is prepared to ask for clarification on an item from the previous reading, but another student asks instead. Crisis averted. Later in class, they find they understand more of the material because of the class discussion and the professor's clarification, and they offer a comment as part of the discussion. They leave even more satisfied than after their Psychology class.

3:00–3:10 p.m. Jamie is the secretary for the Anime club, and they send out emails to the other execs and the general membership reminding them of the upcoming club meeting.

3:10–4:30 p.m. Jamie heads to the gym to run on the elliptical since they are feeling bloated. After running, they take a shower and get dressed again.

4:30–6:00 p.m. This is Jamie's prime study time: the residence halls are often quiet at this time, and their roommate is out of the room as well. They start the reading for their two classes that meet tomorrow: Biology and French. Biology always takes longer to read than French, so they start out reading Biology for an hour, then switch to French. They will return to both subjects after dinner.

6:15–6:50 p.m. Dinner in the dining hall. After eating, Jamie spends time in the cafeteria chatting with friends and picks up a chai tea from the coffee shop.

7:00–8:00 p.m. This is gaming time to prepare for a World of Warcraft tournament being held in their residence hall later in the week. Jamie and their roommate are half of a team.

8:00–8:30 p.m. Prime social media time. Jamie contacts a friend from high school who had a birthday today.

8:30–9:15 p.m. Time spent hanging out with friends in the residence halls and on tasks Jamie doesn't even remember.

9:15–10:30 p.m. Returns to their room to work on Biology homework. Forgets to text parents to tell them things are okay.

10:30–11:00 p.m. Takes a break in the residence hall lounge while popping popcorn and watches the last part of a movie.

11:00 p.m.–12:15 a.m. Finishes French reading and homework assignment due the next day. After more social media time, Jamie heads to their room, with lights out at 1:00 a.m.

Analyzing Your Student's Typical Day

Lots of things happened during this day. First, Jamie attended every class on their schedule which, while not impressive, is something to note. Second, they found time throughout the day to perform academic activities. These included reading over notes from the previous day for a course they're not confident in, reading ahead for the next day, and looking for feedback from a faculty member. Jamie also exercised, spent time with friends, demonstrated they're involved in clubs, and interacted with a wide variety of people in their residence hall.[4] They also watched a measured amount of television and posted on and read social media. In short, they performed many of the same tasks they would do while living in your home.

In terms of their academics, they spent more than five hours in academic pursuits outside of class, which puts them right in line with what many students do daily. And as you can see, they didn't get overburdened by studying for four to six hours straight. Instead, they broke up the time into chunks, noted where they needed to ask for clarification in class, and found that by attending class, they learned things they otherwise wouldn't know—one reason for going to class in the first place! Jamie also took part in the class discussion in at least two of their classes, showing their engagement in the material.

Yes, they went to bed far too late for your tastes and got up late as well. They also skipped breakfast, which isn't great. However, many students stock granola bars or a bit of fruit in their rooms to munch on while walking to their first class if it's after breakfast.

Did anything about this day surprise you? It's a typical day for a college student. I didn't include such things as phone calls home, which most students also make regularly, nor other maintenance activities such as straightening their room, washing their clothes, and so forth. Students sprinkle these tasks throughout the week. I didn't include a student employee position, either, but these are always scheduled outside of their class time. It's also common for students to work on their homework while at their campus jobs, depending on the tasks they have to complete on any given day.

Ask your student about their typical day to understand how college differs from high school. It might surprise them that you asked, but if you learn how they spend their time and discover what they do each day outside of classes, it may make you more comfortable.

Jamie also did what many students do—spend a lot of time interacting with other people, be they folks in the same residence hall, people in the cafeteria, or even people in the recreation center, not to mention current and longstanding friends on social media. Your student is likely to connect with people from a variety of backgrounds on campus, and that is one of the great things about going away to college—the ability to learn more about other people and form meaningful connections with them.

In Brief

Your student may have a schedule that is far different from the one they followed in high school.

They will need to devote significantly more time out of class to academic activities such as reading, studying, and research than in high school.

Finding balance is important for college students. Help them build a weekly schedule that includes physical activity, eating, sleeping properly, and socializing with other students.

Your student has all the time they need to be academically successful and to participate in the other activities they want to. Help them see that.

References

1. McKoon, K. (2011, November 29). Review of *A Day in the Life of a College Student*. CollegeXpress.com. https://www.collegexpress.com/articles-and-advice/student-life/articles/living-campus/day-life-college-student/; Review of *What Does a Typical College Class Schedule Look Like?*

2. (2021). Campusexplorer.com. https://www.campusexplorer.com/college-advice-tips/8BB2B355/What-Does-a-Typical-College-Class-Schedule-Look-Like/

3. Talley, F. J. (2019, February 18). *Taking Control of Their Time as College Students*. Helping Your College Student Succeed. http://www.collegeandparents.com/2019/02/18/taking-control-of-their-time-as-new-college-students/

4. Pranabudi, I. (2014). *Get Familiar With Typical Daily Life at a U.S. College*. U.S. News & World Report. https://www.usnews.com/education/blogs/international-student-counsel/2014/07/22/get-familiar-with-typical-daily-life-at-a-us-college

Chapter 14 - Beyond the Classroom

As I've mentioned before, your student has lots of time in college outside of class. Over fifty hours of that time is dedicated to homework, reading, studying, writing, and similar tasks. But with one hundred sixty-eight hours in a week, what does your student do with the rest of their time?

Assume they sleep an average of six or seven hours per night, and maybe longer on the weekends. That still leaves sixty-nine hours for the week. If we remove two hours per day for meals, or fourteen hours, that leaves fifty-five. How your student uses those fifty-five hours can make or break their college experience.[1]

What Students Can Do on Campus

Something we should remember is that students don't always make the best choices when organizing their time.[2] While obvious to any parent or teacher, the adolescent brain doesn't mature and begin making consistent adult choices until the age of twenty-five.[3] For the traditional-aged college student, that's *after* college. Ever wonder why former military people often do so well in college?[4] It isn't just because they've had training during their military experience: it's the fact that they're six years older and more mature. Ask any noncommissioned officer in the military who works with eighteen-year-old recruits: they may mature while they're in the military, but those first few months are hell on the people who work with them.

The people who work in student affairs at your student's college help students make more mature choices on campus and develop healthy learning experiences outside the classroom. These activities round out your student's experience and help keep their lives balanced and engaging. Student Affairs professionals also keep enjoyment in mind, so your student develops as a young adult but can still have the fun they crave as a "kid."

Clubs and Organizations

Another way that students use their time is in clubs and organizations. Common clubs colleges offer include: anime club, BACCHUS (Boosting Alcohol Consciousness Concerning the Health of University Students), Black Student Union, economics club, environmental club, fashion club, gaming society, InterVarsity Christian Fellowship, programming board or committee, rugby club, Student Government Association, and the list goes on. It's not uncommon for a college or university to offer more than one hundred clubs, so students have many options. Students can learn about clubs during what many colleges call "Club Fair," with each club staffing tables to recruit new members. It's often the liveliest event on campus after orientation.[1,5]

These clubs and organizations may help your student become passionate about a field they never even knew existed, and they may change their major to pursue it. Other students will learn new skills they might never have been able to pursue at home, such as sailing. They'll make lifelong friends within these clubs, since the people they're meeting share similar interests with them.[6] When your student joins a campus club, ask them about how they're enjoying those activities when you ask about their classes. This demonstrates that you understand that their out-of-class activities matter to them and that they contribute to their overall learning in college. If they're not involved in any clubs, that should be a yellow flag to you. When students aren't involved in anything outside of their classes and studying, something is likely wrong, or they aren't adjusting to campus the way they should.

Leadership Opportunities

Along with the clubs and organizations your student may join, many colleges offer leadership opportunities for students. Some of these are obvious and I've mentioned them before, such as Resident

Assistants in the residence halls (or Commuter Assistants for colleges with large commuter populations!), Orientation Leaders, and members of advisory groups to departments, schools, and colleges within a university. These are often coveted, competitive positions, and students are paid for some of them.[7] The scholars program I directed offered opportunities for students to become full-year mentors, working with first-year students as they face the challenges of transitioning to college. We also had mentors for our first-year seminar classes and for our Summer Bridge program. Other universities have similar positions, such as Peer Educators, Peer Counselors/ Advisors, and members of college or university committees. In these committees, students are full voting members, along with staff and faculty members, wrestling with issues such as setting tuition, communications, admissions and marketing practices, and what majors the school will offer.[8] Should your student compete for one of these positions—and be chosen or elected—they will have an excellent opportunity to test themselves as they learn leadership skills. They will also strengthen their connection to the school and increase their chances of graduating on time. Plus, they'll build meaningful connections with faculty and staff members, trustees, and alumni, which can help them in their future careers.

Student involvement on campus isn't just fun and games, though having fun while learning is the best of both worlds. On the whole, however, when your student is involved in a moderate number of activities, they'll increase their chances of graduating on time and be much happier in college.[9]

In Brief

Being successful in college is about more than going to class and studying. Help your student maximize their time out of class as well.

Students can also pursue and find a new major or career based on their out-of-class activities.

References

1. Hawkins, A. (2010). *Relationship between Undergraduate Student Activity and Academic Performance* [Master's thesis.

2. Talley, F. J. (2019, February 18). *Taking Control of Their Time as College Students*. Helping Your College Student Succeed. http://www.collegeandparents.com/2019/02/18/taking-control-of-their-time-as-new-college-students/

3. *Teen Brain: Behavior, Problem Solving, and Decision Making*. (2019). American Academy of Child and Adolescent Psychiatry. https://www.aacap.org/aacap/families_and_youth/facts_for_familie s/fff-guide/the-teen-brain-behavior-problem-solving-and-decision-making-095.aspx

4. Altman, G. (2017, February 24). Review of *Study: Vets Do Better in College Than Comparable Civilians*. Rebootcamp.militarytimes.com. https://rebootcamp.militarytimes.com/education-transition/education/2017/02/24/study-vets-do-better-in-college-than-comparable-civilians/

5. Hawkins, *Relationship between Undergraduate Student Activity and Academic Performance; Get Better Grades in Community College by Being Social*. (n.d.). Community College Review. https://www.communitycollegereview.com/blog/get-better-grades-in-community-college-by-being-social

6. Skogerboe, L. (n.d.). *The Benefits of Joining Student Organizations*. College Raptor Blog. https://www.collegeraptor.com/find-colleges/articles/student-life/5-reasons-join-student-organization/

7. *12 Opportunities for Leadership in College*. (2019). ThoughtCo. https://www.thoughtco.com/opportunities-for-leadership-in-college-793360

8. *7 Ways to Boost Leadership Skills in College*. (2017, September 3). Transizion. https://www.transizion.com/boost-leadership-skills-college/

9. Talley, F. J. (2020, November 29). *Student Involvement Is Important*. Helping Your College Student Succeed. http://www.collegeandparents.com/2020/11/29/student-involvement-is-important/

Chapter 15 - Intercollegiate Athletics

Many of your students participated in high school sports and want to continue while in college. Athletics are a great way to become connected to a supportive community that can follow and support your student throughout their time in college. This must be balanced, however, with the significant demands athletics requires of students. It's important to note here that the vast majority of college students (like above 99 percent) will not play in professional leagues after graduation. Even elite athletes within the most prestigious Division I universities finish their playing careers in college, not the pros.[1,2] Impress upon your student that they should attend college as preparation for a "normal" life, not assuming they will play their sport professionally into adulthood. If your student is really that good, and is heading to a competitive NCAA Division I basketball or football program, you already know about college athletics. But for the rest of you, here are some facts about intercollegiate athletics.

The Student Athlete

Student athletes should understand that they are attending college to earn a degree that will provide them with the skills to chart their career as teachers, physicians, accountants, and so forth, not as people who can play soccer exceptionally well. Putting academics first means spending the same time as other students do on their academics—thirty-five to forty (or more) hours a week—besides practices and game times, which can total twenty hours or more per week. If anything is going "to go" in terms of your student's time commitments, it shouldn't be academics.[2] And since their second priority is often their sport, what they miss out on most is time with friends and, sometimes, sleep. If you ever wondered why student athletes spend most of their time with other student athletes—especially in their sport—this is why. I've traveled with my volleyball team to away matches occasionally, and the students spend most of the trip to and from the events (and often before they warm up) studying.

National Organizations

Most college sports are governed by one of three national organizations These groups provide the rules and policies all member schools follow as they compete and are designed to offer a level playing field for competition.[3] The largest of these is the NCAA—the National Collegiate Athletic Association. There are nearly twelve hundred schools in the NCAA separated into three divisions: Divisions I, II and III.[4] If you follow college sports on television, you're likely following Division I athletics, since they're the ones with the money and status to be covered by television networks. Television networks are unlikely to spend the money to cover Division III athletic contests because they don't get the advertising revenue to pay for it. Division I programs are generally at the largest schools with the largest athletic programs. And these programs may be lucrative. For example, in thirty-nine states, the highest paid public employee isn't a governor or university president—it's a university coach.[5] Plus, for a very thin edge of universities, athletics can provide lots of money to support other programs,[6] but this is not the case for the vast majority of programs.

For most colleges and universities, athletics are an expense, not a source of income. So, why offer athletics in the first place, given what it costs to equip, train, supervise, and transport athletes? The reason is simple: athletics offer options, leadership opportunities, and learning opportunities for students. They're also a way to build cohesion and spirit within the student body. If a college believed their athletic program was a significant drain and not an asset, they'd eliminate some of their programs.

NCAA Division I programs usually offer financial aid to their student athletes as partial tuition, full tuition, or full-ride scholarships. In this way, programs recruit the finest high school athletes so they can build a winning athletic tradition. There are some exceptions to this, however. The Ivy League schools such as Columbia and the University of Pennsylvania don't offer any athletic scholarships, yet they are in Division I.[7]

NCAA Division II includes schools of varying sizes, and if they offer athletic scholarships at all, they offer fewer scholarships than Division I schools. They offer these scholarships for the same reasons Division I schools do: to recruit the student athletes they want to build or strengthen a program. Division III programs—usually at smaller institutions—offer no athletic aid. They exist solely for the other reasons I mentioned above and offer student athletes a balanced educational and athletic experience. But student athletes at every level of the NCAA want to be competitive in their sport and work hard and reap the benefits of their time and effort. I've yet to meet a student athlete who didn't put the work in to make their next game better than the last. And those few who don't won't play much.

The NCAA isn't the only organization governing college sports. The NAIA, or National Association for Intercollegiate Athletics, is an organization of smaller and often independent schools that play outside of the NCAA. They may offer athletic scholarships and at least one source suggests that NAIA aid amounts are similar to those provided by NCAA Division II schools.[3]

The National Junior College Athletic Association (NJCAA) governs community college athletics. Students who prefer to stay close to home take part in NJCAA athletics before transferring to complete their bachelor's degrees. Many athletes start in community colleges so they can attend smaller classes with more academic support before transferring to Division I schools.

Student athletes at every level benefit from participating in sports. Encourage your student to do their homework to select an athletic program that fits their interests and follow the recruiting guidelines on the college website to ensure they don't make a costly mistake when contacting or speaking with coaches. While the coaches are the ones who are held liable for most violations, your student may suffer consequences as well.

When to Quit

You might wonder when college athletes should stop competing. First, your student should stop playing if they have a serious injury. Only a tiny number of college athletes will ever play at the professional level, so playing through an injury is unwise.

Another good reason—and the reason many student athletes quit—is that it stops being fun. College athletes spend a significant amount of their time maintaining their competitive edge. When students don't feel the time investment is worth it anymore, or if they aren't happy playing, they should quit.

Name, Image, and Likeness Payments

A new innovation in college athletics is the concept of name, image, and likeness. Even though all college athletes are amateurs, some universities use athlete photos to bring in revenue, such as for elite football or basketball teams. The NCAA decided in 2021 that athletes in all three divisions can now have control over their name, image, and likeness and can receive payments for them, so long as they follow applicable state laws.[8] This applies both to current and future athletes. This is a significant change, and many believe the NCAA dragged its feet on this for years to avoid "pay for play"—the idea that student athletes should be paid as employees. This concession on name, image, and likeness is an important compromise that may help some student athletes financially. In fact, it may be the most significant thing to happen to intercollegiate athletics as the adoption of Title IX in 1981.[9]

Student athletes who want to receive endorsements or other funds must follow all state laws that apply to them and also avoid violating other NCAA rules. For example, student athletes shouldn't receive any kind of payment from athletic boosters. Further, endorsement deals shouldn't influence athletic recruiting, though that is easier said that done.[9] For those of you who have student athletes who are of the caliber where this matters, please familiarize yourself with NCAA rules on name, image, and likeness and make sure you and your student follow state laws as well. If they don't, they may find their college athletic career derailed before it starts.

The Bottom Line for Athletics

Intercollegiate athletics should be a positive adjunct to the college education your student receives, and this should be the case even at the NCAA Division I level.[2,10] Make sure that your student makes the student part of "student athlete" predominant. That will serve their needs into the future far more than the athletic side. And if you're wondering if you ought to attend your student's college games, please do! The stands are seldom full, except for big-time sports. Your attendance can give a boost to your student's team. And that makes you part of the action as well.

In Brief

Help your student emphasize the "student" part of "student athlete." This is especially important because only a tiny number of college athletes ever play at the professional level.

Student athletes spend a significant amount of their time on their sport while in college, even at the Division III level. Make sure your student knows that going in.

Scholarships for student athletes are only offered at certain levels in the NCAA, NAIA, or NCJAA. And even then, scholarship aid may not cover everything.

Have your student follow all of the recruiting guidelines for their sport and division. You don't want them to miss an opportunity or be penalized for committing a violation.

References

1. *College Athletes Greatly Overestimate Their Chances of Playing Professionally*. (2015). Inside Higher Ed. https://www.insidehighered.com/news/2015/01/27/college-athletes-greatly-overestimate-their-chances-playing-professionally;

2. Hyman, J. S., & Jacobs, L. F. (2014). *8 Tips for the Student Athlete*. US News & World Report. https://www.usnews.com/education/blogs/professors-guide/2010/03/24/8-tips-for-the-student-athlete

3. White, M. (n.d.). Review of *Understanding College Athletic Divisions*. Love to Know. https://college.lovetoknow.com/campus-life/college-football-rankings-explained

4. vcortez. (2016, January 7). *Our Three Divisions*. NCAA. https://www.ncaa.org/about/resources/media-center/ncaa-101/our-three-divisions

5. AB Staff. (2018, June 28). *The Highest Paid Public Employee in 39 States Is a Coach*. Athletic Business. https://www.athleticbusiness.com/college/the-highest-paid-public-employees-in-39-states-is-a-coach.html

6. Writers, S. (2020, November 16). *Do Colleges Make Money From Athletics?* BestColleges. https://www.bestcolleges.com/blog/do-college-sports-make-money/

7. *Prospective Athlete Information*. (n.d.). Ivyleague.com. https://ivyleague.com/sports/2017/7/28/information-psa-index.aspx

8. Hosick, M. (2021, June 30). NCAA Adopts Interim Name, Image and Likeness Policy. NCAA. https://www.ncaa.org/news/2021/6/30/ncaa-adopts-interim-name-image-and-likeness-policy.aspx

9. Tully, J., & Rorabaugh, D. (2021, July 1). *What Does the Term NIL Mean and Why Is It So Important to College Sports?* Palm Beach Post. https://www.palmbeachpost.com/story/sports/college/2021/07/01/what-does-nil-mean-ncaa-college-sports-name-image-likeness/7819355002/

10. Hyman & Jacobs, *8 Tips for the Student Athlete; Fundamentals of the Student-Athlete Experience*. (2012, June 13). Majeski Athletic Consulting. https://www.majeskiathleticconsulting.com/fundamentals-of-the-student-athlete-experience/

Chapter 16 - Helping Them Adult on Campus

The student who walks the halls of a college or university is not a kid, however young they may appear. As they enter college, they are adults and will be treated that way by the college administration and faculty. This transition can be tough. Think back to the first time you bought a car on your own. You had to figure out what you could afford and determine the monthly costs, maintenance, and car insurance bill. If you walked into the dealership by yourself without your parents, you were probably nervous. When I secured a loan to purchase a washer and dryer many years ago—my first ever loan—I was on pins and needles. I was certain something would derail what I thought of as a reasonable request. When I got the loan, I couldn't hide my joy in doing something on my own that was so "adult-like." A colleague only two years older than me dashed that when he said, "F. J., a signature loan for $850 from the credit union isn't a big deal." Well, thanks a lot, bud, for deflating *that* balloon.

Performing tasks like purchasing a car, renting an apartment, buying insurance, making your own appointments to see a doctor or dentist—these are adult things we all do. Yet for our first-year traditional-aged college students, they're new. That's the challenge of what we refer to as "adulting" on campus.[1,2] And as their family member, you can help them make this transition successfully. They can become students who stand out among their peers and are respected by both staff and faculty.

Let Them Take Initiative

The first place they need to be adults is within the classroom. Attending class, paying attention to the syllabus, and taking part in class discussions shows the faculty your student is serious about their education.³ When students have even the remotest doubt about something in class, they should ask about it, either during class or faculty office hours. Students who are adulting also challenge professors if their opinion differs from theirs. They are open to feedback—both positive and negative. Encourage your student to ask their professors how they can improve and have them follow the advice. Faculty notice this.

That same level of initiative applies to other offices on campus. When your student has a bill that's due, they should visit the business office and ask about it. Sure, they can call you for clarification afterward, or even while they're in the office, but it's their responsibility to stop by the office to learn what they need to do.

Having said this, I encourage students to call their parents while they're in the financial aid office, since they're unlikely to know much of the information the financial aid office needs from them.⁴ They should ask the financial aid person if they can call you for information while they're in the office, but even if they call you, your student should still take the lead. They should ask many of the questions, and you should step in only when the student is lost. At the end of the meeting, ask what else the financial aid office needs you to do, and make sure you get it either to the office or to your student. The financial aid official will be impressed if the student remains active in the conversation rather than just turning the entire conversation over to you. I refer to this as calling for a lifeline. Encourage your student to say to a staff person, "I don't quite understand that part of the bill. Would you mind if I called my folks, since they may know more about this than I do?" Asked in that way, the student isn't abdicating their responsibility, they are calling in an important resource.

Students should also learn how to go "up the chain" to get things done. This often gets a bad rap, because it evokes the "I'm going to call your manager" scenario. But going up the chain prompts students to raise questions with one person then go to that person's supervisor if not satisfied: that's how many organizations work.⁵ It doesn't help their cause to go to the president of their college because of a food allergy or the lack of vegan options, because all the president will do is direct the student to the appropriate person to address their concern. If the student starts at the proper place, they may get their problem resolved without calling in the cavalry. News flash: *you* are the cavalry, and you shouldn't be called in to intervene unless there is a really big deal or emergency.

Let's play out the vegan options in the cafeteria scenario. Your student may have been led to believe the vegan options would be broader than they are. They should speak with the director of food service before they speak to the president. They may be able to speak directly with the executive chef and find them quite open to trying out new recipes. In addition, many food service operations have an advisory group of students, staff, and faculty who work on dining options, and they may ask your student to join. That's a win-win. But if your student starts with the president or a vice president, who then mandates that the chef speak with them, the chef will listen to your student's concerns, and may even take positive action, but won't offer your student a chance to join the advisory group. Sure, your student had a minor win, but they could have been more successful had they started at the right place.

Facilitate When Needed

However, you can facilitate things. This may prevent a situation from getting worse in serious circumstances. During our daughter's first year in college, a student she'd graduated with from high school died while at his college. There was no foul play, and I don't recall the reason he died, but you can imagine the grief many students felt. My wife called the area coordinator—the professional staff person—for our daughter's residence hall and told him what happened so he would know. He strolled through the residence hall that day and happened upon our daughter. While chatting with her, she told him what happened, and he offered his support. She appreciated receiving this support from him without even asking for it. This may be one reason she applied for and served as an RA for the next three years. Yes, her mother helped her get the support, but she helped *by activating the existing support system on campus.*

Consider the Source of Information

An additional challenge of adulting on campus is that students may see faculty and staff as the enemy, and they are less likely to want to approach them for help—even though that's their job. Instead, they turn to older students—sophomores, juniors, and seniors—for advice. It's no surprise that their advice can be either very good or very bad, and your student may not know the difference. Help them "adult" by asking them how they know the advice they're receiving from other students is any good. Asking them to evaluate the value or accuracy of the information they receive from others is an excellent way to strengthen their adulting skills.

Let Them Figure It Out

Another way we help them 'adult" is by not helping them. You may be one of many who receive that phone call late on Saturday night from your student wanting to come home.[6,7] They don't like their roommate, the faculty hate them, no one listens to them, and they don't have any friends. We help our students by listening to them, offering support, and showing our confidence that they can succeed in school. We don't help them succeed by getting in the car and moving them home the next day. Sure, we can and should call them the next day and chat after they are off the ledge, so to speak. But rushing to solve their problems isn't what happens with adults. (And don't even think about calling the roommate to ask why they're being a jerk to your student.) Adults challenge inappropriate behavior by others, offer compromises, and look for solutions to what bugs them. In other words, they seek a Plan B. Being an adult is often about developing a Plan B, be it for a job they didn't get, a boss who's hard to work with, and so forth. As adults, we are so accustomed to our Plan Bs we don't even realize we're using one. But our students' lives have often been a straight line from elementary school to middle school to high school and then to college. When something challenges that straight line, they're often floored and get thrown off their game. Yet as college juniors, the same issue that completely derailed them as a first-year student doesn't even register.

You can also role-play with them. For example, if they're planning to speak with a department chair about an issue, such as getting into a closed class or a professor's unfair grading, you can role-play by serving as the department chair so they can practice what they'll say. This is just like a practice job interview. This gives your student practice in how adults conduct business and get things done. And even if the result of the meeting isn't what they hoped for, debrief with them afterward and offer your support. With your support and wise counsel, your student will learn how to navigate the challenges of young adulthood on campus.

When You Visit Campus

When you visit campus (and you should!) remember that you are a respected guest in your student's new home. You have several opportunities to visit, the most common being parent/family weekend.[8]

I encourage you to take part in this, at least during your student's first year in college. Parent/family weekend often includes several programs and activities for both you and your student, and it's also an excuse to see them, which you're likely dying to do. But while you're there, observe a few ground rules.

First, this is your student's home. They should be the ones to take the lead in the activities you participate in, and they should set the tone of your interactions. This doesn't mean you can't be yourself, but be mindful of what your student is interested in doing. If you happen to see another parent you met during orientation, feel free to connect with them.

Second, if you need to visit a campus office, such as the business, financial aid, or food service office, let your student take the lead. They should be the one to make formal requests of the office with you as their backup.

While on campus, get to know your student's entire new home, so ask what off-campus spots they visit. For our daughter, there were two diners—one right across from campus and the other about two miles away—that she liked to frequent.[9] We made a point of visiting each of these when we'd stop by, and we purchased gift certificates to the one across from campus as one of her Christmas presents every year. She and her friends appreciated it.

And speaking of those friends, if you're on campus and their roommate or another friend doesn't have their parents on campus, take them to dinner. It won't cost you much, but it supports your student and their friends, and that goes a long way toward keeping your student connected with their new community. [8,9]

Another great benefit of taking part in special weekends is the chance to see the growth in your student. My wife and I were amazed during our daughter's first parent/family weekend, with how many people spoke with her, asking to meet us. Our daughter had made a mark on that campus, and seeing that made us much more relaxed about her future there. She was becoming an adult, and the confidence we gained by seeing her in action confirmed that she was going to be fine.

In Brief

College students often find it hard to handle life as young adults rather than as big children. Help them make that transition and give them "adulting" tips along the way.

Encourage your student to ask questions in class and engage actively in class discussions with their professors. This can make all the difference for them.

Even when they call you for a lifeline, such as when they're visiting a campus office, help them take the lead in working with the office, with your assistance and guidance.

Remember, you can still contact their university if you need to—just do this sparingly.

Sometimes, the best way to help your student is not to help them, forcing them to make important choices and follow through on their own. Give them the space to do that.

References

1. *Actually, We Do Deserve Accolades for Adulting*. (2020, March 5). Greatist. https://greatist.com/grow/adulting-meaning-validation;

2. Talley, F. J. (2018, July 6). *First Time for Everything*. Helping Your College Student Succeed. http://www.collegeandparents.com/2018/07/06/first-time-for-everything/

3. Talley, F. J. (2018, September 4). *The Syllabus*. Helping Your College Student Succeed. http://www.collegeandparents.com/2018/09/04/the-syllabus/

4. Talley, F. J. (2018, July 6). *Whose Financial Aid Is It Anyway?* Helping Your College Student Succeed. http://www.collegeandparents.com/2018/07/06/whose-financial-aid-is-it-anyway/

5. *Problems with Services on Campus*. (n.d.). The NCCSD Clearinghouse and Resource Library. https://www.nccsdclearinghouse.org/problems-with-services.html

6. Talley, F. J. (2019, September 27). *Homesickness*. Helping Your College Student Succeed. http://www.collegeandparents.com/2019/09/27/homesickness/

7. *Homesickness In College—Freshman Advice*. (2020, May 2). University of the People. https://www.uopeople.edu/blog/homesickness-in-college

8. Talley, F. J. (2018, September 18). *Parent and Family Weekend: Do You Go?* Helping Your College Student Succeed. http://www.collegeandparents.com/2018/09/18/parent-and-family-weekend/

9. *Visiting Your College Student*. (2016, September 23). Collegiate Parent. https://www.collegiateparent.com/parent-blog/visiting-your-college-student/

Chapter 17 - Finding Help in College

The students most likely to succeed in college—in my opinion—are those who are willing to ask for *and* accept help.[1] In fact, something I ask my students the first time I meet them is: "On a scale of one to ten, with one being you never ask and ten being you always ask, how likely are you to ask for help in class? How about out of class?" I tell students I want them to be an eight for both answers—or at least for one of them. The reason is simple: we know that college is much more challenging than high school. Students who recognize that and take the risk of asking for help and accepting it will succeed. Those who try to power through the tough material without asking for guidance often don't.

This may seem odd to you. Don't we assume most college students are capable of doing the work or, in the vernacular of high schools and school districts, that they are "college ready"? Well, yes and no. The students have the intellectual ability to succeed in college, but sharpening those skills to make them successful in college is the tough part. This requires learning new skills and being open to unlearning nonadaptive skills. This makes the difference for entering students.

Every parent or other family member worries that their student will need help adjusting to the campus but that the help they need won't be available. But I've found the opposite to be true: the resources are waiting to be deployed, but the students don't access them.[2] Colleges and universities offer support services of every type to their students. For example, most colleges offer some counseling or advising services to help students when they face difficult mental or emotional challenges.[1,3] Colleges also routinely offer tutoring or other supports for their students. The problem these departments report time and time again is that students access their services either when it's too late or when they are too emotionally drained to continue. Please help your student avoid this.

The Wellness Wheel

Many colleges and universities use the wellness model to show how they define being healthy and happy on campus. The welless model used by most college and univeresities seeks a balance among eight interconnected dimensions, namely:

- Emotional
- Spiritual
- Physical
- Environmental
- Financial
- Social
- Intellectual
- Occupational

The model suggests that when the dimensions on the edge of the wheel are in balance, your student will be successful. Consider the following: What if your student is so focused on their academics that they neglect their health? Or what if they isolate themselves so much from other people that they find they have no motivation to pursue their goals? Balance within the wellness wheel is the key to everything.

Academic Support

Your student can take advantage of several support services. First, if they had either a 504 plan or an IEP (Individualized Educational Plan) in high school, they may be eligible for accommodations in college.[4] Eligible means just that: some students may not be eligible because the accommodations they received in high school aren't appropriate for the college setting. Also, accommodations aren't dumbing down the curriculum. Think of it this way. I wear glasses now, and one fantastic tool that I've used at times is large-print books so I can read the material more easily and avoid eye fatigue. Accommodations are like large-print books: they level the playing field. Accommodations do not give the students receiving them an advantage—they eliminate a disadvantage they have that others often can't see.

Tutoring is another valuable service. Since college courses move much faster than high school courses (three to four times faster!), students may fall behind and need additional time or teaching to catch up.[5] Tutoring offered either by successful students or by professionals is a way to bridge the gap for your student. Many schools also offer writing centers where students can receive help writing thesis statements and with self-editing. The center staff—be they highly qualified students or professionals—may also review drafts so students can master college writing assignments. The goal for both tutoring and writing centers is for students to learn new skills so they won't need that same level of tutoring or writing help in later courses, but if they do, the center will help them.[6]

Study groups are another great tool some colleges offer. Study groups harness the collective brainpower of a small group of students to help each other learn.[7] I've worked at several universities where I might walk by the student cafeteria or snack bar on the way to a meeting. Every once in a while, I'd see four students sitting in a booth, quizzing each other on their course material. I enjoyed seeing students engaging with each other like that, and I would often walk by two or three times. Watching students engage in their learning without a faculty member standing over them is one of the most satisfying things an educator can see. These students were using the power of the study group method to improve their performance. I wrote and published a guide that explains study groups in detail: that's linked in this book's appendix.

When They Stumble Academically

Please keep in mind that your student may stumble academically.[8] This may take the form of failing an exam or a course, or perhaps doing poorly enough during a semester that they find themselves on academic probation. Students and parents see this as a failure. I see probation as an opportunity to assess what went wrong and make the necessary corrections. Students who have been reluctant to ask for help in the past start asking for help when they're on probation because they have to. Think of it as the stick rather than the carrot approach to improve their academic performance. If your student ends up on probation, ask them what their plan to improve is and how their college can help them. Offer any help or reflection you can, and if the plan your student gives you is to "work harder," nod and say, "I'm sure you will, because this is important to you, but how are you going to make sure you follow through on that?" This may get you a snippy response from your student, and you can back off then. Understand, though, that their snippiness isn't because they're mad at you: they're angry at themselves for not succeeding. Return to the discussion when tensions are lower and help develop or outline a realistic plan they can follow. This is also the time to pull out the list of contacts you wrote down during spring orientation so you can direct your student to the specific offices and people on campus where they can get help.

Mental and Physical Health

Most college students who visit their college's counseling center aren't going because of significant psychological problems. Some may experience depression or more serious mental challenges, but most students visit the counseling center for other reasons. They may be sad about a family member who died, have difficulty getting along with their roommate, or feel alone because they haven't made as many friends as they thought they would. These conditions are normal, and you should encourage your student to visit the counseling center to get the perspective and help they need.[9] Helping students handle these challenges is what the office is for, however small or large their challenges may seem.

The same thing applies to physical health. If your student has a sore throat, they should go to the wellness center, because they may have something like strep for which they can get treatment, rather than thinking it's just a cold. These centers are staffed by people who put the student first and who will do what they can to reduce the mental, emotional, and physical challenges to your student's success. Encourage your student to use these services when they need to; remember, you are paying for them as part of tuition.

Advising and Career Development

The biggest mistake many students make is to visit the career center for the first time in the middle of their senior year. Career centers at most colleges cry out for students to visit in their first year so they can help the students map out their upcoming four years and prepare for their careers.[10] For example, students benefit tremendously from having practical experience in their field of choice before graduating from college. This could take the form of interning in a company for a few weeks or shadowing a professional in the field so they know what to expect. These experiences—whether they are short-term or last a full semester—give students a leg up and a renewed sense of purpose about their career long before they seek their first professional job. For others, their first practical experience in their field of choice shows them that a particular career is not for them. In either case, learning that early on is valuable.

Academic advising is another area that students ignore outside of getting advice about classes once per term. Smart students go to their academic advisors to get help designing a preferred course sequence that prepares them for the career they want, and not just to complete the major.[11] These contacts with advisors may also lead to letters of recommendation when it's time to search for a job.

The network of people willing and able to help your student succeed is larger than you may think. For example, I knew a custodian in a residence hall who got to know the habits of the students on the floors he was assigned to clean. He noticed after a few weeks a guy who used to be in class at 10 a.m. on Monday, Wednesday, and Friday was suddenly in his room playing video games during that time. The custodian asked the student what was up, and his answer was: "I didn't do the reading, so I figured I shouldn't go to class." The custodian told the student that playing video games wasn't good preparation for class either and that he needed to go to class whether he read the material or not. That custodian was as much an educator and mentor as any college professor or advisor. Many people who work at your student's college are as well.

In Brief

Students who are open to ask for and receive help will often succeed in college. Just "toughing it out" without receiving guidance and support along the way seldom works.

Encourage your student to access support services as soon as they feel even remotely lost in class or unable to understand an assignment. Even when students receive help in college, they often ask for it too late.

If your student only talks with you about academics and isn't involved in some kind of student club or social activity, ask them about that. Maintaining a balance in their lives is important and actually supports their academic success.

Students who received accommodations in high school through a 504 Plan or IEP may be eligible for accommodations in college. Make sure your student asks about those before the term begins.

If your student stumbles academically, encourage them to develop a realistic plan for recovery. Just saying they'll "work harder" isn't enough.

References

1. *How to Help Your Child Seek Out Support for Common Problems in College.* (n.d.). www.understood.org. https://www.understood.org/en/school-learning/choosing-starting-school/leaving-high-school/how-to-help-your-child-seek-out-support-for-common-problems-in-college?_ul=1

2. Talley, F. J. (2020, February 21). *Meeting Us At Least Halfway.* Helping Your College Student Succeed. http://www.collegeandparents.com/2020/02/21/getting-students-to-use-student-services-in-college/

3. *How to Help Your Child Seek Out Support for Common Problems in College*; Talley, F. J. (2019, January 29). *Using Their Lifelines: Getting Students to Use Campus Services.* Helping Your College Student Succeed; http://www.collegeandparents.com/2019/01/28/using-their-lifelines-getting-students-to-use-campus-services/

4. *Helping Students with Disabilities Understand Accommodations in College.* (n.d.). Edutopia. https://www.edutopia.org/article/helping-students-disabilities-understand-accommodations-college

5. Nist-Olejnik, S., & Holschuh, J. (2016). *College Rules! How to Study, Survive, and Succeed in College.* Ten Speed Press.

6. Nist-Olejnik & Holschuh, *College Rules!*

7. Hodon, S. (2019, April 12). Review of *How to Ask for and Get Help in College.* CollegeXpress.com. https://www.collegexpress.com/articles-and-advice/student-life/articles/living-campus/how-ask-and-get-help-college/

8. *How to Help Your Child Seek Out Support for Common Problems in College.*

9. Talley, F. J. (2019, September 27). *Homesickness.* Helping Your College Student Succeed. http://www.collegeandparents.com/2019/09/27/homesickness/

10. Talley, F. J. (2020, May 2). *Connecting Your Student to the World of Work.* Helping Your College Student Succeed. http://www.collegeandparents.com/2020/05/02/connecting-your-student-to-the-world-of-work-is-a-priority-for-students-and-families-alike/

11. Talley, F. J. (2020, February 4). *The Best Academic Advising Appointment.* Helping Your College Student Succeed. http://www.collegeandparents.com/2020/02/04/the-best-academic-advising-appointment/

Chapter 18 - Experiential Learning

This chapter focuses on experiential learning. These practical experiences are often housed within the Career Center. Most students need practical experiences in college to be competitive in the job market beyond simply attending the required classes to graduate.[1]

Experiential learning opportunities take many forms, but most are tied to either a major or a career interest the student is exploring. For example, a student interested in becoming an accountant might shadow an accountant and watch what that person does. To go deeper, the student might serve as a paid or unpaid intern during the summer, organizing financial records to prepare for an audit by the accounting form. The student is learning about their potential career field in a practical way that shows the career "behind the curtain" so they can make an informed choice about that in the future.[2]

Internships and Externships

The Eller College of Management at the University of Arizona says that the primary difference between internships and externships is that externships are often unpaid and help students explore careers, generally in a more surface-level way.[3] Internships are often undertaken when the student is well into their major and preparing for the formal transition to the world of work. Many colleges now refer to externships as shadowing programs, to further differentiate them from internships.[4] Both internships and externships place students into professional work settings and give them exposure to that career field.

Cooperative Education

Another long-term approach to career preparation is known as cooperative education. In the traditional co-op program, students may attend school for two terms in classes and then work full time for an academic term. This means that it may take them five years or more to graduate, but cooperative education helps them in several ways.[5] First, they earn money to help defray the costs of tuition. Second, they gain valuable work experience in their fields, which makes the transition to a lifelong career much easier. Cooperative education students often find full-time employment opportunities at the company where they co-op, so they slide into those opportunities easily—and with a level of seniority no other recent graduate will have. Several schools have made cooperative education a significant part of their curriculum, such as Northeastern University in Boston, Rochester Institute of Technology, and Drexel University in Philadelphia.

Students can gain an edge through practical experience in other ways, too. I've worked at several colleges that tout the amount of research their students can engage in at the undergraduate level. If your student connects with a faculty member and works within the behavioral science lab or in researching water quality, encourage them to follow through about opportunities to expand their knowledge. These experiences distinguish students who have taken their education deeper from those who have only scratched the surface.[6]

The same applies to service-learning opportunities. Service learning refers to participating in service activities that are part of a class or course design.[7] For example, students in an accounting course learn accounting principles, IRS schedules, and so forth in class but then put their knowledge to the test by helping senior citizens complete their taxes. This genuine work experience helps the accounting students learn how to apply their skills and to work more successfully with a client base. They wouldn't get this from the accounting course alone. Students who take part in service-learning courses often report that their learning "came alive" by applying it in actual work situations. When they engage in a service activity that is tied to their classroom activities, they also reflect on both the learning and impact of that service as part of the course, that is an example of service learning. Service learning is at the interaction of learning, service, and reflection.

Students in courses that emphasize learning and service will later reflect on how that service helped them and likely have a better idea of what their future careers might look like. This is what service learning can do for your student.

We can also encourage students to follow their passion by pursuing projects such as writing original musical or theater works or drafting a business plan as part of their education. Sometimes these activities occur as part of a course, or they may be part of a student organization or professional association. When your student engages in their learning in this way, they further show potential employers how they have already developed important job-related skills in problem solving, developing and implementing projects, and so forth. These are the skills employers often say are lacking in recent college graduates. By showing this kind of experience, your student shows they're more than ready to start their professional career.

In Brief

Practical experience—often in the form of internships or externships—may be invaluable in giving your student experience they can use when finding a job or pursuing graduate study.

Cooperative education is another model that provides students with practical experiences—and often income—to support their education.

Another great option for students to gain academic and job-related experience is through research opportunities at their university. Encourage them to look for those.

References

1. *10 Ways to Build Job Skills in College*. (n.d.). Princeton Review. https://www.princetonreview.com/college-advice/experiential-learning-opportunities

2. Talley, F. J. (2020, May 2). *Connecting Your Student to the World of Work*. Helping Your College Student Succeed.

http://www.collegeandparents.com/2020/05/02/connecting-your-student-to-the-world-of-work-is-a-priority-for-students-and-families-alike/

3. *Externships vs Internships*. (2020, June 12). Eller College of Management. https://eller.arizona.edu/news/2020/06/externships-vs-internships

4. Talley, *Connecting Your Student to the World of Work*.

5. *Undergraduate Co-op*. (2020, April 30). Steinbright Career Development Center. https://drexel.edu/scdc/co-op/undergraduate/

6. Moody, J. (2014). *Why Undergraduate Research Matters in College*. US News & World Report. https://www.usnews.com/education/best-colleges/articles/2019-09-20/why-undergraduate-research-matters-in-college

7. *What Is Service-Learning?* (n.d.). Suffolk University. https://www.suffolk.edu/student-life/student-involvement/community-public-service/service-learning/what-is-service-learning

Chapter 19 - Study Abroad

Study abroad is a wonderful opportunity for students to leave campus to study in another country for a semester or a year. There are also shorter-term programs in which students visit other countries for a week to a few weeks while enrolled in a specific course related to that country. Colleges and universities have offered such programs for decades, and some pride themselves on the number of their students who study abroad.[1,2]

For example, Arcadia University near Philadelphia has a program called Preview.[3] To take part in Preview, first-year or transfer students take a two-credit course in the spring of their first year at the university. These courses are focused on another country in the world. When our daughter was a first-year student, she had several options to choose from. Her top three in order were Oman, South Africa, and Tuscany. She researched Oman extensively during the spring semester and then spent nine days in the country to complete her research along with twenty other students. Arcadia is ranked highly in study abroad participation by its students for programs like Preview.

Why Study Abroad?

Some students are interested in an international studies career. This is why one of my daughter's best friends—she was an international studies major—traveled to two different countries during her junior year. For other students, studying abroad is the opportunity to get outside their comfort zone. And let's face it: how many of us have wanted to travel the world? That's much harder to do once you're working a full-time job, but easy to do while in college. Neither my wife nor I studied aboard while in college and we regret it.

Students benefit tremendously from studying abroad. First, they often develop excellent language skills, which gives them an advantage in the job market. A second benefit is the chance to test themselves in an unfamiliar environment. Students studying abroad have the opportunity to experience a new culture up close and see parts of the world most people will never experience, and at a much deeper level than a tourist might experience.[4,5] This experience also gives students something to discuss during job interviews. If they can discuss how they've developed and matured through their international experiences, many employers choose to invest in a risk-taking graduate and hire them.

Graduate schools often view study abroad in the same way. Someone who has studied abroad successfully is often better prepared to handle the rigors of graduate study because they've remained academically successful while navigating an unfamiliar culture, language, and so forth. Students also report making lifelong friends while they are abroad, building solid ties with people in other countries.[5]

I recommend study abroad highly as you can see. And it's important to note that the cost often isn't very high. In fact, most forms of financial aid a student receives can apply to semester-long or full-year study abroad programs.[6] The only added charges for studying abroad are transportation, visa fees, and spending money. While that is a net increase in expense, imagine staying for four months in Rome, South Africa, or Costa Rica and spending only an additional $2,000, while earning fifteen college credits! People may spend $2,000 (or more!) for a week on vacation, so study abroad is a bargain.

A shorter-term option—known as the study tour—is a brief stay in a country that helps students dip their toes in the study abroad universe.[7] While these are often lower risk for students, they may cost more. For example, a student may travel with a professor to Peru to study the ruins of Machu Picchu. That's a great opportunity, but check out the costs. Often the student fees have to cover the cost of the instructor's travel. In addition, the out-of-pocket costs might rival or even be higher than for studying abroad for a semester, and financial aid rarely covers those costs. Students choose a study tour for a shorter experience or because they feel they can't leave family or a job for an entire semester. And while this is not my preferred choice, if it's all the student can do, I do recommend a study tour.

National Student Exchange

A less-known program but still valuable experience is National Student Exchange (NSE). Traveling from Maryland to Montana may not seem as appealing as studying abroad, yet students who take part in NSE often report the same experience of immersion in another culture given the wide range of environments and cultures within the United States.[8] NSE includes schools from forty-nine states (Delaware was the only holdout in 2020), seven Canadian provinces, plus Puerto Rico, the U.S. Virgin Islands, and Guam. Students from any of these institutions are eligible to attend classes, as visiting students, at other member schools through a matching system. The kicker is that only students from member schools can participate in the exchange, and that number is not as large as I'd like it to be. But for students from one of these schools, imagine traveling from Mississippi State University to spend a semester at the University of Regina or the University Alaska, Fairbanks.

With the exception of learning a new language, students participate in NSE for the same reasons they choose to study abroad. Exceptions to this are Puerto Rico and some campuses in Quebec, where they may need to use a different language. And the potential for maintaining friendships and networking with the people they meet is higher for NSE participants. While lesser known than traditional study aboard, I am a big proponent of the NSE program.

In Brief

Students who study abroad while in college often report that the experience was life changing. Also, they often find studying abroad helps them prepare for adulthood and for the independence of graduate school. Student in any major may benefit from participating in study abroad.

Federal and state financial aid can often support students who study abroad for a semester or a year but may not support shorter-term experiences like study tours. Students should check out all the options before they select a study abroad experience.

National Student Exchange—a lesser-known option for students—gives students valuable experiences at other domestic universities. For students who choose not to leave the county—or can't—NSE is a great option.

References

1. *American Colleges with the Best Study Abroad Opportunities: These International Programs Are Incredible—Best Value Schools.* (2020, July 21). Best Value Schools. https://www.bestvalueschools.com/rankings/study-abroad-colleges/;

2. *Universities Where Most Students Study Abroad.* (2021). U.S. News & World Report. https://www.usnews.com/best-colleges/rankings/most-study-abroad

3. *Preview Broadens My Perspective of the World* (n.d.). Arcadia University. https://www.arcadia.edu/blogs/because-arcadia/post/preview-broadens-my-perspective-world

4. *Why Study Abroad?* (2017, June 5). USA Study Abroad. https://studyabroad.state.gov/value-study-abroad/why-study-abroad;

5. *10 Benefits to Studying Abroad | Study Abroad Guide.* (2019). International Student. https://www.internationalstudent.com/study-abroad/guide/ten-benefits-to-studying-abroad/

6. *Federal Student Aid.* (n.d.). Studentaid.gov. https://studentaid.gov/understand-aid/types/international

7. *Faculty-Led Study Tours.* (n.d.). Endicott College. https://studyabroad.endicott.edu/index.cfm?FuseAction=Abroad.ViewLink&Parent_ID=0&Link_ID=BC957EC1-A4BA-DB3E-035EF4256C259073

8. *National Student Exchange.* (n.d.). https://www.nse.org/

Chapter 20 - Alternate Paths

Parents of college students often worry if their student chose the right school. If not, the saying goes, they may be forced to transfer to find a better match. I'd love to tell you that won't happen to your student, but I can't. In fact, some students realize they're at the wrong college, and many of those students will leave. That needn't be a tragedy, nor should it hurt them. Finding the right school after a poor match is great for a student who then finds the right combination of people, majors, atmosphere, and so forth and takes off academically.

I should have transferred from my undergraduate college, since it was never a good match for me. I tried in the middle of my sophomore year, but during that fall, the school I wanted to attend closed their fall term admissions in November, and I only got serious about transferring in December. Since that school was out, I stayed put. This was during the era when students lost many more credits when transferring than is the case today.[1] Well, I stayed, graduated, and moved on to graduate school, but your student shouldn't have to suck it up as I did.

Why Transfer?

Transferring schools is finding or revisiting the right match between student and school. Remember when we discussed using items such as major, proximity to home, and campus "feel" to determine match? Well, what if your student attends School X and finds it's great when they're a biology major but not as good for an environmental studies major—which is the major they switched to? One of my students transferred from my college to another because she wanted to pursue a major in linguistics, which our college didn't offer. A change of major is one good reason to transfer.[1]

Campus atmosphere is another good reason. If your student doesn't care for fraternity and sorority life and attends a school where fraternities and sororities are a big thing, they may not be comfortable. The same applies to people who are looking for what Greek life provides and their current college *doesn't* offer that. Remember, it's about each individual student—your student—not an ideal vision either you or I may have about the perfect college.

When your student brings up the possibility of transferring, ask what's led them to that decision. Did a particular incident cause this? What were they looking for in the first school that they didn't have, and could they make that happen at their current school? And it's okay to ask how they plan to graduate within a reasonable time if they transfer since they may still lose *some* credits depending on where they transfer. These are reasonable questions. Resist the urge to get angry, saying things such as "we can only afford to pay for four years so you need to stick it out here."[2,3] Mind you, that may be true, but focusing only on the money won't help your student make the best choice. I've seen time and time again where students remain at the wrong college. Some flounder, while others graduate, but they're so bruised by that time, their overall college experience is negative. Since their only focus has been on finishing college, they've gained nothing positive from the experience. So, please hold the financial concerns—as valid as they are—aside for the moment.

If the answers to the questions above suggest that your student is making a snap decision—such as being unhappy about a roommate and faculty member who prompted your student to declare they just can't "do college"—you can help them make a better and more mature decision. (Note: if those *are* the reasons, direct them to the people who can resolve their concerns and help them stay in school!)

If you believe their reasons for transferring are valid and reasonable, their next step is to research other institutions, looking at department ratings, and figure how their credits will transfer.[4] Visiting the campus is a must since they're risking more now than when they were in high school. Ask the same questions about faculty, atmosphere, curriculum, and so forth you asked before, but expect more concrete and clearer examples and answers from your student. Ask questions such as: "What's going to be different about this school and how will they fit in? How will they approach being a transfer when colleges often give transfers less guidance, yet expect them to perform like other sophomores or juniors?"[5]

Many states have online systems students can use to evaluate their credits and see how their credits will likely transfer. Suggest that your student download a copy of their transcript and examine the catalog of the potential new school to see how their courses might transfer. In some states, a student who has earned an associate degree enters a four-year college as a junior, with most or all of their general educational courses waived. And since transfer is expected for community college students, they offer lots of resources to help their students make that transition.[6] Many community colleges also have agreements between their school and the four-year schools their students transfer to.[7] These are known as articulation agreements. These help students choose courses at the community college that will transfer successfully to school A or school B within their state. This makes the students' transition to their four-year college of choice much smoother. And if they really want to attend University X and there is a transfer coordinator at their school who works with University X, your student should consult with that individual—along with their academic advisor—before selecting their courses to be sure they'll transfer. That's an inside tip.

Withdrawing or Taking a Leave of Absence

Sometimes, a student just needs to stop out of school for a while. This may be because of an illness—theirs or yours—or hitting a wall academically. This allows them to take a semester off to take stock, review their goals, and either come back renewed or change their school or career choice. Every parent I know dreads their student stopping out because it's often seen as giving up and letting go of their dreams.[8] Others, however, use their leave of absence to refocus their energies, mature as young adults, and return to college ready to excel. If your student is worn out by a tough semester and doesn't appear ready to continue, a leave of absence might be wise. The same applies if they had surgery and returning too early might compromise their recovery or their academic success. A leave of absence is often granted with the understanding that the student will return to school within a semester or a year.[9] If your student is considering a leave of absence, discourage them from worrying about graduating with their peers; that doesn't matter. Encourage them instead to use their time away from college analyzing and reflecting so when they make their next decision, it's the right one.

Withdrawing means leaving that school for good. Sometimes students withdraw to transfer, but others simply decide college is not for them. Some students may return to an earlier passion for a skilled trade like auto mechanics or an occupation like farming. For those students, using what they've learned in college in their new career may be enough for them.[10] Withdrawal is not a bad thing for some students, but it can be the wrong decision for students who could have thrived given the right circumstances. As a family member, show them understanding and compassion as they navigate this decision.

Finally, be sure your student observes all the deadlines for either returning to school or transferring. If they are transferring to another school, make sure they honor all the deadlines and follow them so they are successful. Students taking a leave of absence should know that most colleges require students to show their intent to return or finish their leave of absence by certain dates. The last thing a college wants is for your student to decide to return with renewed energy and commitment and find they missed the deadline.[11]

I'd also suggest taking a course at another college during their leave to keep their hand in the game and also to try out that college before transferring. That may not be possible, and taking a course online isn't the same thing as attending an in-person course. But it may still be of value.

If we remember that college is a marathon and not a sprint, the stresses often associated with transferring, withdrawing, or taking a leave of absence can be reduced. For many students, one of these may be the right choice.

In Brief

Students may choose to leave their university either for a period of time, called a leave of absence, or completely. This happens for many good reasons, but it's best to check with your student and ask why they're choosing to leave. It's possible they may be able to stay at their school with the right support.

Some good reasons to change schools are a change of major, a new life circumstance—such as a marriage—or a clear recognition that the student is in the wrong school.

What students should not do is to transfer schools or withdraw from college altogether for something that could be resolved easily, such as a roommate conflict or a particularly difficult course or challenging professor. If that's why your student wants to leave school, urge them to resolve the real problem first.

Continue to monitor the process of finding a second school; your student should still be in the driver's seat, but you may need to keep them properly focused on what's really important.

If their reason for a leave of absence or withdrawing concerns their mental health, help them get the support they need so they may be able to return to college.

A leave of absence or temporary stop doesn't mean they can't return to college in the future. Help them leave that door open.

References

1. Friedman, J., & Moody, J. (2015). *Transferring Colleges: 10 Frequently Asked Questions*. US News & World Report. https://www.usnews.com/education/best-colleges/articles/2017-09-22/transferring-colleges-10-frequently-asked-questions

2. Friedman & Moody, *Transferring Colleges*.

3. *Guide to Transferring Colleges*. (n.d.). Princeton Review. https://www.princetonreview.com/college-advice/transferring-colleges; *How Does Transferring Colleges Work?* (2019, December 27). Road2College. https://www.road2college.com/tips-for-students-transferring

4. *Guide to Transferring Colleges.*

5. Mitchell, T., & Moody, J. (2014). *9 Things College Transfer Students Need to Know.* US News & World Report. https://www.usnews.com/education/best-colleges/slideshows/10-things-prospective-college-transfer-students-need-to-know

6. *How Does Transferring Colleges Work?*

7. *What Is an Articulation Agreement?* (n.d.). CollegeTransfer.net. https://www.collegetransfer.net/AskCT/What-is-an-Articulation-Agreement

8. *Taking a Leave of Absence: What You Need to Know.* (n.d.). Mental Health America. https://www.mhanational.org/taking-leave-absence-what-you-need-know

9. *Taking a Leave of Absence*; Lucier, K. L. (2019). *Helpful Tips for Withdrawing From College.* ThoughtCo. https://www.thoughtco.com/how-to-withdraw-from-college-793147

10. Clendenon, M. (2016, September 14). *Should You Take a Leave of Absence from College?* Student Caffé Blog. http://blog.studentcaffe.com/take-leave-absence

11. Lucier, *Helpful Tips for Withdrawing From College.*

Chapter 21 - After College

It's no surprise to parents that four years goes by quickly, though it may surprise your student. Their years in college are only a small part of their lives. Encourage them to enjoy their time in college as they prepare to join the full-time workforce. But they shouldn't wait until April of their senior year to prepare for that life.

The Career Center

I've talked about career centers before, and I've mentioned that the one thing my career center colleagues always tell me is they want to meet with students sooner than their senior year.[1] The stereotype is that students will show up at the center in April of senior year and ask for help in finding a job. That's not the best way to secure a position that meets the students' needs and gives them the career and life choices they want. This takes time and lots of practice.[2]

Schools that nudge, push, or require students to visit their career centers in their first years are ahead of the game. With an ever-changing economy and the memory of earlier economic downturns, getting them to the career center isn't the hard sell it might have been ten or twenty years ago. And if your career center doesn't encourage first-year students to visit them, your student shouldn't attend that school, since that school is way behind the times.[3] First-year students in a career center might work on resumes for a campus or off-campus job, take part in alumni receptions, and begin shadowing programs. Career centers also help students learn how to work toward a career using both their academic and nonacademic activities.[4]

Here's an example: a student who wants to work in higher education, perhaps to become a dean of students, often starts by being an RA.

This position provides them a great introduction to the work of student affairs professionals. Those students can point to the RA part of their resumes so graduate schools and employers can see what they can do. Their career center can help them incorporate the experience into their resume.[5]

Young Professionals

One goal for you as a family member is to help your student act and work like a young professional as early as possible. This means encouraging them to spend time with faculty in their major, including attending lectures by those individuals.[6] They should also participate in department activities that bring faculty members and students together. These faculty members may be the gatekeepers for summer opportunities such as internships and research experiences in college. When faculty members know your student, they're more likely to offer them these opportunities. Several of my students have connected with their faculty early like this, and as a result, each took part in significant summer and research experiences in psychology and in neuroscience. One of them met with the coordinator of the neuroscience program during her first semester and crafted her major and minor then. While some students thought she had jumped the gun, she immersed herself from the beginning in what would become her career and had a lot of meaningful experiences throughout college.

Welcoming Your New Professional

I won't talk about how to find a job, since career advisors can explain that process far better than I can. They can also teach your student the tools they need to thrive as they seek full-time employment. But once they transition into their first job, your student may need your help in approaching their work as young professionals rather than as students.[7]

Help them live small by living either at home or in a smaller place so they can save money. Most graduating seniors don't know how much it costs to live independently, and many find it overwhelming. Encourage them to consider a small yet safe place to live where they have easy access to necessities such as food and their job.[8] The same applies to cars. If they need to buy a car, I'd encourage them to buy used at first because of the lower initial cost and the lower cost of insurance. Leasing may also be an option depending on the deal and on features such as mileage charges.[9]

Could your new professional live at home and save money? For some of us, the answer is yes since we want them close anyway. In addition, it helps them save money, particularly if they are paying off student loans. If they live at home, reset your relationship, since they'll have new habits and working hours. Approach this as if they are a new tenant rather than your son or daughter.[10] Map out how you want to interact with them and what your mutual expectations are. Be open to discuss things such as overnight visits, room and board charges, food purchasing, and household chores. This living arrangement is unlikely to be long term, but for many students, it's a wise financial strategy.

While they are living as new professionals in your home or elsewhere, help them build a budget, putting aside money for savings, utilities, insurance, and so forth and guide them with decisions on new tasks such as taking out a car loan. For most graduating seniors, these are tasks they have never considered: your help is crucial.

In fact, serve as a mentor to them the same way you might to a new professional in your workplace.[11] In this way, you'll be reminded you are working as adult/adult, rather than adult/child. Encourage your student to find mentors at work as well.

Your student may also experience college withdrawal, especially when they start paying bills. They may also be bored since their work is unlikely to take as much time overall as college did. When I left graduate school and took a regular nine-to-five job, I was bored to tears. I solved that by getting a new and more challenging position. Many recent graduates are overwhelmed, though, by the complexity of their work and the responsibility but bored when they aren't working. Help your student build a balanced life outside of work.

The Ultimate High

I've told students for years that the two best times are when they show up at orientation and when they cross the stage at graduation.

I'm one of the few people I know who loves wearing a cap and gown, regardless of how hot they can be in the spring and summer. My cap and gown represent my commitment to working with young people who've just reached the highest accomplishment of their lives in an environment that stretches them in ways they never thought they could. Yet they thrive, and they succeed. Seeing your student reach these heights is a heady experience, and I urge you to cherish the feelings and the images it provides. This is one of our ultimate rewards as family members, and you had a share in this success.

In Brief

Urge your student to remember to visit the career center long before their last term in college. As soon as your student meets with them, the career center can help.

Students who would like to attend graduate school should connect with faculty in their discipline right away. That gives them the best chance for research opportunities, lab assistant positions, and so forth that will pave the way for graduate school.

Once your student graduates, help them make that transition: it may be as difficult as the transition from high school to college. Help them with budgeting, payment plans for their student loans, and newer tasks such as car loans. They'll need this guidance and will likely appreciate your help.

Mentor your young professional, the same way you would a younger employee on the job. It's all part of our lifetime role as parents.

Good luck!

References

1. Talley, F. J. (2020, May 2). *Connecting Your Student to the World of Work*. Helping Your College Student Succeed. http://www.collegeandparents.com/2020/05/02/connecting-your-student-to-the-world-of-work-is-a-priority-for-students-and-families-alike/

2. Writers, S. (2018, November 14). *How to Use Career Centers to Advance Your Career*. LearnHowToBecome.org.

https://www.learnhowtobecome.org/career-resource-center/making-the-most-of-career-centers/

3. Talley, *Connecting Your Student to the World of Work.*

4. Writers, *How to Use Career Centers to Advance Your Career*; Talley, F. J. (2018, July 6). *Questions for Your Admissions Counselor.* Helping Your College Student Succeed. http://www.collegeandparents.com/2018/07/06/questions-for-your-admissions-counselor/

5. Koenig, R. (2018). *How to Make the Most of Your College Career Center.* US News & World Report. https://money.usnews.com/money/careers/applying-for-a-job/articles/2018-03-12/how-to-make-the-most-of-your-college-career-center

6. Writers, *How to Use Career Centers to Advance Your Career.*

7. *How Parents Can Help the Transition From College to Career.* (2016, April 19). Jody Michael Associates. https://www.jodymichael.com/blog/childs-first-job-college-5-ways-parents-can-ease-transition/

8. *Tips for Your Young Adult and Their 1st Apartment.* (n.d.). Simplyfamilymagazine.com. https://simplyfamilymagazine.com/tips-for-your-young-adult-and-their-1st-apartment

9. Bartlett, J. S. (n.d.). *How to Buy Your First New or Used Car.* Consumer Reports. https://www.consumerreports.org/buying-a-car/how-to-buy-your-first-new-or-used-car/

10. *10 Guidelines for Millennials Living at Home.* (2010, July 16). All Pro Dad. https://www.allprodad.com/10-guidelines-young-adult-child-moves-home/

11. Pozin, I. (2012, August 30). *Why Young Professionals Need Mentors for Success.* HuffPost. https://www.huffpost.com/entry/why-young-professionals-n_b_1842738

Appendix

Thanks for reading Parenting a College Student! As promised, here are two valuable resources for you.

In Chapter 11, I promised a form which includes 24 hours a day for students to schedule their time.

Here's the link to the document in Google Drive: **https://tinyurl.com/24-hourschedule**

You can also access the form through this QR Code:

Some years ago, I wrote a study group booklet while working at my local community college. Here's the link: **https://tinyurl.com/Study-Group-Guide-2023**

You may also access the form through this QR Code:

Meet the Author

F. J. Talley is an educator whose career has spanned four decades. He was privileged to work at educational institutions in six states in both the public and independent sectors. His career began in Student Affairs, but he also taught undergraduate Psychology courses at two schools, and graduate courses in Student Personnel and Higher Education at Rowan University. His well-rounded college administration career included positions as Dean of Students, Associate Provost, and Vice President, in addition to serving as President of a small college.

He was highly successful as director of a scholars' program at an honors college, in helping underrepresented students succeed. During an eight-year period, underrepresented students at the college boasted a four-year graduation rate 71%–higher than the graduation rate of other students, which was also higher than the four-year graduation rates of all but 10 public colleges in the United States.

His goal through CollegeandParents.com is to help students succeed and to give parents the tools to help them.

Also by F. J. Talley

Flight of the Raven
Twin World
Desert Son

Standalone

Take Hart
21 Things Parents Wish They Knew
Before Their Kids Went Off to College

Watch for more at collegeandparents.com and fjtalley.com

www.ingramcontent.com/pod-product-compliance
Lightning Source LLC
Chambersburg PA
CBHW020423010526
44118CB00010B/385